The Living Land of Lincoln

At the Lincoln home, Springfield, Illinois.
(Photo: Fred J. Maroon/Louis Mercier)

The Living Land of Lincoln

a celebration of
our 16th President
and his abiding
presence... in
photographs,
with text by

THOMAS FLEMING

READER'S DIGEST PRESS

McGRAW-HILL BOOK COMPANY
New York St. Louis San Francisco
London Toronto Mexico
Dusseldorf

Library of Congress Cataloging in Publication Data
Fleming, Thomas J
    The living land of Lincoln.
    1. Lincoln, Abraham, Pres. U. S., 1809–1865.
2. Presidents—United States—Biography. I. Title.
E457.F56   973.7′092′4 [B]   80–13381
ISBN 0-07-021297-X

Grateful acknowledgment is hereby made to the following organizations and individuals for permission to reprint material from the following sources:

Harper & Row Inc. for *In The Footsteps of the Lincolns* by Ida M. Tarbell, copyright © 1924 by Harper & Brothers, renewed 1952 by Sarah A. Tarbell and John Newlin Trainor; *With Malice Toward None* by Stephen B. Oates, copyright © 1977 by Stephen B. Oates, Harper & Row Inc.; *Reminiscences of Lincoln,* Allen T. Rice, ed., copyright © 1885 by Allen Thorndike Rice, renewed 1888 by Allen Thorndike Rice, Harper & Brothers, 1909; *Mary, Wife of Lincoln* by Katherine Helm, copyright © 1928 by Katherine Helm, Harper & Brothers, 1928; *Intimate Character Sketches of Abraham Lincoln* by Henry B. Rankin, copyright © 1924 by J. B. Lippincott Co.; and *In the Lincoln Country* by Rexford Newcomb, copyright © 1928 by J. B. Lippincott Co. The preceding selections are all by permission of Harper & Row Publishers Inc.; Abraham Lincoln Association for "Environs of Lincoln's Youth" by Louis A. Warren, Abraham Lincoln Association Papers, 1936; "Lincoln's Humor" by Benjamin P. Thomas, Abraham Lincoln Association Papers, 1936; "Lincoln: Self Biographer" by Paul M. Angle, *Abraham Lincoln Quarterly,* September 1940, No. 3; "A. Lincoln: His House" by A. L. Bowen, Lincoln Centennial Association Papers, 1925; "Lincoln's New Salem" by Benjamin P. Thomas, Abraham Lincoln Association, 1934; "Lincoln's Genius of Places" by Carl Sandburg, Lincoln Association Papers, 1933; G. P. Putnam's Sons for *Abraham Lincoln: A New Portrait* by Henry B. Kranz. Copyright © 1959 by Henry B. Kranz. Reprinted by permission of G. P. Putnam's Sons; Appleton-Century-Crofts for *Lincoln's Youth* by Louis A. Warren, Appleton-Century-Crofts, 1959; Public Affairs Press for *Lincoln's Boyhood* by Francis M. Van Natter, Public Affairs Press, 1963; Mrs. Paul M. Angle and Mrs. Earl S. Miers for *The Living Lincoln* by Paul Angle and Earl S. Miers, eds., Rutgers University Press, 1955; Holt, Rinehart & Winston for *A. Lincoln, Prairie Lawyer* by John J. Duff. Copyright © 1960 by John J. Duff. Reprinted by permission of Holt, Rinehart & Winston, Publishers; Viking Press for *Lincoln Talks* by Emmanuel Hertz. Copyright © 1939 The Viking Press, Inc., renewed 1967 by The Viking Press. Reprinted by permission of Viking Penguin Inc.; Scarecrow Press for *Abraham Lincoln and Coles County, Illinois* by Charles H. Coleman (Metuchen, N.J.: Scarecrow Press, 1955). Copyright © 1955 by Charles H. Coleman; *The Lincoln Herald* for "Mr. Lincoln's Light From Under A Bushel," by Richard A. Lufkin, Winter 1953 and "This Side of the Mountains: Abraham Lincoln's 1848 Visit to Massachusetts," Summer 1978, *The Lincoln Herald,* Lincoln Museum of Lincoln Memorial University, Harrogate, Tennessee; Houghton Mifflin Company for *Abraham Lincoln in New Hampshire* by Edwin L. Page, Houghton Mifflin 1929; and *Abraham Lincoln* by Albert J. Beveridge, Houghton Mifflin, 1928; Illinois State Historical Society for *Illinois As Lincoln Knew It: A Boston Reporter's Record Of A Trip in 1847,* edited by Harry E. Pratt, from *Transactions of the Illinois State Historical Society,* 1937; Dodd, Mead for *Lincoln and the Railroads* by John W. Starr, 1927, reprinted by permission of Dodd, Mead & Company, Inc.; Little, Brown and Co. for *Mary Lincoln* by Ruth P. Randall, 1953; The University of Chicago Press for *Lincoln's Last Speech In Springfield In the Campaign of 1858,* edited by Oliver R. Barrett, copyright © 1925 by The University of Chicago, by permission of the University of Chicago Press; Coward, McCann & Geoghegan Inc. for *Abraham Lincoln Goes To New York* by Andrew A. Freeman, copyright © 1960 by Andrew A. Freeman, reprinted by permission of Curtis Brown Ltd.; William Morrow & Co. for *West Point* by Thomas Fleming. Copyright © 1969 by Thomas Fleming. By permission of William Morrow & Co. Inc.; Books For Libraries Inc. for *Abraham Lincoln By Some Men Who Knew Him,* Paul M. Angle, ed., Books For Libraries Press, 1969; *Magazine of History* for "With Lincoln At Gettysburg" by Junius B. Remensnyder, *Magazine of History,* Vol. 32, no. 125–6.; Manchester, New Hampshire Historic Association for *A History* compiled by George Waldo Browne, published by the Amoskeag Manufacturing Company, 1915; Times Books for *Abraham Lincoln, A Press Portrait* by Herbert Mitgang, copyright © 1971 by Herbert Mitgang. Reprinted by permission of *Times Books,* A Division of Quadrangle/The New York Times Co., Inc. Massachusetts Historical Society for "Letter Written By Augustus Clark Recounting the Assassination of Lincoln," copyright © 1977 the Massachusetts Historical Society; Peter Smith Publisher Inc. for *Myths After Lincoln* by Lloyd Lewis, Press of the Reader's Club, 1929. Bobbs-Merrill Co. Inc. for *Personal Recollections of Abraham Lincoln,* by Robert W. McBride, Bobbs-Merrill, 1926; and *Lincoln At Gettysburg,* by William E. Barton, Bobbs-Merrill, 1930.

CHAPTER ONE

Lincoln still lives in the land he loved.

The land still lives in the story of Lincoln's life.

These are the two ideas that have shaped this book. With the camera's dramatic eye, we have roamed America to find the landscapes and buildings that have remained unchanged since the days when Lincoln himself looked upon them. To enlarge these images, we have added to them a web of personal observation by a wide range of men and women. Some knew Lincoln in his lifetime. Others have made significant contributions to our vision of Lincoln in works of scholarship, fiction, and poetry. To these, we have added words from Lincoln's own lips and pen. Out of this verbal and visual experience we hope readers will emerge with a deeper kinship not only with the man himself, Abraham Lincoln in his humor, his pathos, his wisdom, but also with the essential America that lived in his tall frame.

You may be surprised to learn how much of America came within range of Lincoln's eyes. Farmer, riverman, storekeeper, state assemblyman, circuit riding lawyer, congressman, senatorial and presidential candidate, Abraham Lincoln was always a man on the move. He was also the son of a restless pioneer. The result was a life with far more traveling in it than most people associate with Lincoln. Twice he flatboated down the Mississippi to New Orleans. He stood on the promontory at Council Bluffs, Iowa, and gazed westward along the railroad route that would span the continent. He stumped Kansas, Ohio, Wisconsin. He inspected the textile factories of Manchester, New Hampshire, and admired the foaming thunder of Niagara Falls. He spoke in Trenton, New Jersey, and in Independence Hall in Philadelphia. He visited the Five Points, the worst slums of 1860 New York. He walked with mournful eyes through the streets of devastated Richmond.

The America that Lincoln knew best—and that lives most vividly in his life—was the Kentucky-Indiana-Illinois heartland where he was born and grew to manhood and maturity. It was here that he acquired what Carl Sandburg called "Lincoln's genius of places." To understand this gift, we must begin with a visit to

Enlargement from the broken glass plate original life negative of Lincoln taken by Anthony Berger at Brady's Washington gallery, April 20, 1864, for artist Frank Carpenter. In 1956 it was presented by Carpenter's grandson, Emerson Carpenter Ives, of Pawling, N.Y. to Lloyd Ostendorf, and is now in Ostendorf's collection in Dayton, Ohio.

Lincoln's 1809 birthplace on the Big South Fork of Nolin's Creek (now the Nolin River) about three miles south of present-day Hodgenville, Kentucky.

Early in this century Lincoln admirers enshrined his first log cabin home in a Greek temple, a decision which stirred considerable controversy. One of Lincoln's biographers, Ida Tarbell, approached the place in a rather critical mood—which soon changed.

When I learned that it had been decided to build upon the farm a Greek temple, I shrank from the idea. I did not know what should be done, but in my ignorance it seemed to me that they were doing what should not be done.

You approach the monument by a winding driveway, on each side of which the natural growth of the land has been left, all the beautiful and varied growths of this part of Kentucky. A place of gorgeous color in the clear sunlight of a perfect October morning. My first visit was on one of the loveliest of October days.

The little temple stands on a rising slope of ground—exquisitely white, small, serene—approached by a long, broad, generous stairway of marble. It is a triumph of perfection. Its proportions are right, its size is right. The landscape gardening simply protects the drive, the staircase, the temple itself from the encroachment of the woods, leaving the natural setting undisturbed. It is a joyful thing to see.

But in the exultation of finding it so beautiful, I dreaded an entrance. Would not the little cabin seem mean? Would not its placing inside this perfect thing make it ridiculous by contrast?

The beauty and the wonder of it is [*sic*] that it is not so. It somehow belongs. Why, I do not know; but it stands there so simply—a thing without pretension, but of an extraordinary dignity in its simplicity. You have only the native log structure, the clay chimney; but every stone of the chimney, every timber of the cabin is there because it was needed. Never have I been so impressed with the dignity of the thing which fits the need.

In these surroundings, one visualizes with wonderful sympathy and clearness the little Lincoln family in their one room home. This cabin sat on a rising slope,

8

Early in this century Lincoln admirers enshrined his first log cabin home in a Greek temple, a decision which stirred considerable controversy. (Photo: Douglas Fowley)

with the same lovely surroundings that you may see to-day—trees of every kind, vines underbrush, fruit. Nancy [Lincoln] and her children on the doorstep at even-time looked out on as beautiful a place as heart could wish.[1]

Another more matter-of-fact visitor noted the farm's main characteristics.

The cave spring close by the cabin site and the old oak which marks the beginning corner of the farm are the only two unusual contributions which nature has made to Lincoln's birthplace, unless it be the "red earth" which is characteristic of the soil in that part of Kentucky.[2]

This colorful soil and the landscape of the farm inspired one of the best passages in a famous poem about Lincoln.

The color of the ground was in him, the red
    earth;
The smell and smack of elemental things;
The rectitude and patience of the cliff;
The good-will of the rain that loves all leaves;
The friendly welcome of the wayside well;

The courage of the bird that dares the sea;
The gladness of the wind that shakes the corn;
The mercy of the snow that hides all scars;
The secrecy of streams that make their way
Beneath the mountain to the rifted rock;
That gives as freely to the shrinking flower
As to the great oak flaring to the wind. . . .[3]

A ten-year-old cousin, Dennis Hanks, remembered Abraham's birth. He also recalled the elder Lincolns and their hard life on Nolin's Creek.

Pore? We was all pore, them days, but the Lincolns was poorer than anybody. Choppin' trees, an' grubbin' roots, an' splittin' rails, an' huntin' an' trappin' didn't leave Tom no time to put a puncheon floor in his cabin. It was all he could do to git his fambly enough to eat and to kiver 'em. Nancy was turrible ashamed o' the way they lived, but she knowed Tom was doin' his best, an' she wasn't the pesterin' kind nohow. She was purty as a pitcher an' smart as you'd find 'em anywhar. She could read an' write. The Hankses was some smarter'n the Lincolns. Tom thought a heap o' Nancy, an' was as good to her as he knowed how. He didn't drink, or swear, or play cards, or fight; an' them was drinkin', cussin', quarrelsome days.[4]

Thomas Lincoln, Abraham's father, decided the soil was not good enough on the Nolin's Creek farm, and when Abraham was two, the family moved 10 miles to a 230-acre farm on Knob Creek. This was the first home that Lincoln remembered. Still privately owned, the farm contains the cabin of Lincoln's boyhood friend Austin Gollaher, who rescued him from drowning in a pool formed by the creek. The site of the near tragedy is just below a latter-day bridge, its tempting waters still sheltered by trees, as it was in Lincoln's day.[5]

The road running past the farm was one of the main highways of American history—the Louisville–Nashville turnpike. Thousands of pioneers traveled west along it in their canvas-topped wagons, pulled by six and eight teams of straining oxen. Peddlers, politicians, preachers from every sect, even an occasional scientist, such as Christopher Columbus Graham, famed for his studies of Kentucky's flora and fauna, stopped at the Lincolns' door. The growing boy was by no means isolated from the world beyond the horizon of the steep limestone bluffs along Knob Creek.[6]

Young Lincoln did not spend all his time observing travelers. From his cousin we get a vivid picture of Abraham's boyhood life as a young woodsman.

Abe was right out in the woods, about as soon's he was weaned, fishin' in the crick, settin' traps fur rabbits an' muskrats, goin' on coon-hunts with Tom an' me an' the dogs; follerin' up bees to find bee-trees.[7]

It was on this Kentucky farm that Lincoln revealed the sensitive side of his nature. Here is how he told the story to a friend in his later years.

When a boy, six years old, I went over to a neighboring farm. A litter of striped piggies had just been born, and I was so taken with them that they could not get me away from them. The owner filled me with supreme joy by saying: "You may have one of those pigs if you can get him home." I instantly accepted the offer. I had on a tow shirt—one which my mother

11

had woven—reaching below my knees, and fastened at the neck by a wooden button my father had made. Using the front of it as an apron, or sack, I rolled my pig up in it and carried him home.

That pig was my companion. I played with him, and taught him tricks. We used to play hide-and-seek. I can see his little face now, peeking around the corner of the house, to see whether I was coming after him!

After awhile he got too heavy for me to carry around, and then he followed me everywhere—to the barn, to the plowed ground, and to the woods.

When he grew larger, I turned the tables on him, and made him carry me; and he did it just as happily and cheerfully as I ever performed the same service for him. Father fed him corn—piles of it—and how he did eat! He grew large—too large for his own good and mine.

At the table I heard father say he was going to kill the hog the next day. My heart was as heavy as lead. I was seized with a determination to save my playmate. I slipped out and took him with me into the woods. When father found what had happened he yelled as loud as he could:

"You, Abe, fetch back that hog! You, Abe, fetch back that hog!"

The louder father called, the further and faster we went, till we were out of hearing of the voice. We stayed in the woods till night. On returning I was severely scolded. Father and mother explained to me that we could not keep the hog through the winter for me to play with—that hogs were meant to be killed for food. I was not convinced. After a restless night I rose early and slipped out of the house quietly, to get my pig and take him away for another day's hiding. But my father had forestalled me by rising still earlier, and he had fastened my pet in the pen.

I knew then, there was no hope for my pig. I did not eat any breakfast, but started for the woods. I had not got far into the woods before I heard the pig squeal, and I ran faster than ever to get away from the sound.

Being quite hungry at midday, I started for home. Reaching the edge of the clearing, I saw the hog, dressed, hanging from the pole near the barn. I began to blubber.

When Abraham was two, Thomas Lincoln moved the family to a 230-acre farm on Knob Creek. This was the first home that Lincoln remembered. (Photo: Douglas Fowley)

12

I just couldn't reconcile myself to my loss. I could not stand it, and went far back into the woods again, where I found some nuts that satisfied my hunger till night, when I returned home.

The next morning, I went into the yard and saw some of the reminders of the butchering. Taking a big chip, I scraped the scattered blood and hair into a pile and burned it up. Then I found some soft dirt which I carried in the fold of my tow shirt, and strewed it over the ground, to cover up every trace of what was to me an awful tragedy.[8]

Another Lincoln memory of Knob Creek recorded a natural disaster that would soon inspire his father to move again.

Our farm was composed of three fields, which lay in the valley surrounded by high hills and deep gorges. Sometimes when there came a big rain in the hills the water would come down the gorges and spread over the farm. The last thing I remember of doing there was one Saturday afternoon; the other boys planted the corn in what we called the "big field"—it contained seven acres—and I dropped the pumpkin seed. I dropped two seeds every other hill and every other row. The next Sunday morning there came a big rain in the hills; it did not rain a drop in the valley, but the water, coming down through the gorges, washed ground, corn, pumpkin seeds and all clear off the field.[9]

Thomas Lincoln, discouraged by such crop failures and harassed by legal problems about the deed to his farm, decided to move from Kentucky to reportedly better land in southern Indiana. The family rafted across the half-mile-wide Ohio River near the mouth of Anderson Creek and struggled another sixteen miles through thick woods to the bank of Pigeon Creek. The year was 1816. Abraham was seven years old.

The October glory was still on the trees when the little party reached the knoll on the land which Thomas had chosen for them. They could not have known then how really beautiful a site it was. To-day, with the land cleared so that one can look over the great valley, see the line of Pigeon Creek, locate homes of neighbors with whom Abraham was to grow up, identify point after point connected with his life here, you get a very genuine respect for Thomas Lincoln's choice of a site in what was then an unbroken forest. Probably there was nothing to be seen about them but trees, trees of great size, many primeval timber: elms, chinquapin oaks, walnut, maple, birches, sassafras, trees which now were gold and red and yellow; when the sun sifted through them they became things of pure color, almost without substance.

Along the stream there were cleared places covered with crimson sumac and masses of golden rod, wild rose, black-berry vines, an almost impenetrable tangle. Not far away, too, there was what was called a "deer lick," a salty marsh to which wild animals came, a precious neighbor to the settler who must depend upon his gun for his supply of meat.[10]

Years later, in a lively poem about a bear hunt, Lincoln added a vivid glimpse of the Indiana wilderness of 1816.

When first my father settled here
T'was then the frontier line;
The panther's scream, filled night with fear
And bears preyed on the swine.[11]

In a biographical sketch Lincoln wrote in 1860, he recalled the new farm as his introduction to hard work.

He [his father, Thomas] settled in an unbroken forest; and the clearing away of surplus wood was the great task ahead. A., though very young, was large of his age, and had an axe put into his hands almost at once; and from that till within his twenty-third year, he was almost constantly handling that most useful instrument.[12]

The soil was rich along Pigeon Creek, and relatives, including the family of Dennis Hanks, soon joined the Lincolns. Although Abraham had attended school in Kentucky for a few weeks, he got his first serious education at an Indiana school run by Andrew Crawford. His cousin described its impact on him.

Well, me 'n' Abe spelled through Webster's spellin' book twict before he got tired. Then he tuk to writin' on the puncheon floor, the fence rails and the wooden fire-shovel, with a bit o' charcoal. We got some wrappin' paper over to Gentryville, an' I made ink out o' blackberry brier-root an' copperas. Kind o' ornery ink that was. It et the paper into holes. Got so I could cut good pens out o' turkey-buzzard quills. It pestered Tom a heap to have Abe writin' all over everything thataway, but Abe was jist wropped up in it.

"Denny," he sez to me many a time, "look at that, will you? *Abraham Lincoln!* That stands fur me. Don't look a blamed bit like me!" An' he'd stand an' study it a spell. 'Peared to mean a heap to Abe.[13]

A favorite Lincoln story from his Indiana schooldays concerned the custom of reading aloud from the Bible. One of his classmates, named Bud, had not progressed very far in the art of reading. To him fell verse number 12, which contained the names Shadrach, Meshach, and Abed-nego, the Israelites who were thrown into the fiery furnace.

Little Bud stumbled on Shadrach, floundred on Meshach, and went all to pieces on Abed-nego. Instantly the hand of the master dealt him a cuff on the side of the head and left him wailing and blubbering as the next boy in line took up the reading. But before the girl at the end of the line had done reading he had subsided into sniffles and finally became quiet. His blunder and disgrace were forgotten by the others of the class until his turn was approaching to read again. Then, like a thunderclap out of a clear sky, he set up a wail which even alarmed the master, who with rather unusual gentleness inquired, "What's the matter now?"

Pointing with a shaking finger at the verse which a few moments later would fall to him to read, Bud managed to quaver out the answer:

"Look there marster," he cried, "there comes them same damn three fellers again."[14]

In 1818 tragedy entered Lincoln's life. The soil was rich along Pigeon Creek—almost too rich. Lush vegetation and frequent flooding from heavy rains produced mists and fogs that gave the settlers malaria–like fevers. More se-

Interior, Knob Creek.
The road running past the farm
was one of the main highways
of American history—
the Louisville-Nashville turnpike.
(Photo: Douglas Fowley)

In 1816 the family moved again,
to Pigeon Creek in southern Indiana.
In a biographical sketch written
in 1860 Lincoln recalled the new
farm as his introduction to
hard work. (Photo: Douglas Fowley)

rious was a disease that appeared when their cows ate snakeroot, a plant containing a potentially fatal poison. Already weakened by fevers, Nancy Hanks Lincoln succumbed to the "milk sickness," as the pioneers called it, in a few days. While his son and daughter wondered and wept, Tom Lincoln hammered a coffin and dug a grave.

Perhaps a half mile from their cabin was a knoll heavily wooded, uncleared, a spot where probably already a grave or two had been dug. It was October and the woods were in full color, red, yellow, brown. Let us hope it was a sunny day, for the heart-broken little family had little or nothing of that which they felt was due to the dead to comfort them, no burial service, no sympathetic neighbors. They were alone and forlorn in a stricken land.

Tom Lincoln and his children would go often to visit her grave, but they were never able to do more to honor her than to put up what was common in the world at that time, what one sees everywhere still in the old graveyards, an uncut fragment of red sandstone, no lettering, no date, only this marker.[15]

A year after Nancy Hanks Lincoln died, Thomas Lincoln returned to Kentucky and married Sarah Bush Johnston, a widow with three children. He brought her to the cabin in Indiana. Here is what she remembered of Abraham Lincoln's boyhood.

Abe was about 9 years of age when I landed in Indiana. He didn't like physical labor—was diligent for knowledge—wished to know and if pains & labor would get it he was sure to get it.

When old folks were at our house, [he] was a silent and attentive observer, never speaking or asking till they were done and then he must understand everything, even to the smallest thing, minutely and exactly; he would then repeat it over to himself again and again, sometimes in one form and then in another, and when it was fixed in his mind to suit him he became easy and he never lost that fact or his understanding of it.

He would hear sermons . . . come home, take the children out, get on a stump or log and almost repeat it word for word. His father made him quit sometimes, as the men quit their work. . . . I induced my husband to permit Abe to read and study at home. At first he was not easily reconciled to it, but finally he was willing to encourage him to a certain extent. . . .

He was the best boy I ever saw.[16]

His cousin confirms Lincoln's passion for knowledge.

Seems to me now I never seen Abe after he was twelve 'at he didn't have a book some'ere 'round. He'd put a book inside his shirt an' fill his pants pockets with corn dodgers, an' go off to plow or hoe. When noon come he'd set down under a tree, an' read an' eat. An' when he come to the house at night, he'd tilt a cheer back by the chimbly, put his feet on the run, an' set on his backbone and read. Aunt Sairy [Sarah Bush Lincoln] always put a candle on the mantel-piece for him, if she had one. An' as like as not Abe'd eat his supper thar, takin' anything she'd give him that he could gnaw at an' read at the same time. I've seen many a feller come in an' look at him. Abe not knowin' anybody was 'round, an' sneak out ag'in like a cat,

an' say: "Well, I'll be darned!" It didn't seem natural, nohow, to see a feller read like that. Aunt Sairy'd never let the children pester him. She always said Abe was goin' to be a great man some day.[17]

Abraham Lincoln spent fourteen years of his life along Pigeon Creek in southern Indiana's Spencer County. It was there he grew to his full six feet four inches and earned a reputation as a strong man.

By the time Lincoln was seventeen, his muscles were as hard as dornicks. Whenever he appeared at log rollings a joyous whoop went up, for his great strength was an asset to any team. Ten to twenty men gathered at a settler's cabin. With axes and handspikes they went to the deadening ground or clearing. Organizing two teams, they tried to defeat each other in piling the most logs into a mountainous heap. The team that enrolled Abe Lincoln usually won.[18]

He soon became famous for his prowess as a wrestler. In later years he told the artist Thomas D. Jones the secret of his success.

All I had to do was to extend one hand to a man's shoulder, and with weight of body and strength of arms, give him a trip that generally sent him sprawling on the ground.[19]

From boyhood on, Lincoln loved a joke.

One day, Abe bumped his head against the top of the Lincoln door frame and his stepmother said, "Abe, I don't care so much about the mud you track in on my floor for I can scrub that up; but you must be more careful about my whitewashed ceiling."

Patiently waiting until she was away from the cabin, Abe persuaded neighborhood children to wade in a mud puddle. Afterward he led them into the cabin and, one by one, he picked them up and marched them upside down across the spotless whitewashed ceiling. Scarcely had the children fled out of sight before Mrs. Lincoln returned. Wondering what she would do, Abe watched her examine the muddy footprints, drop into a split-bottomed chair and break into a hearty laugh. He started for the door.

Mrs. Lincoln: "Where are you going?" "Wait and see." He went to the lime barrel, mixed a batch of whitewash and re-whitewashed the ceiling, beams and all.[20]

The land left its stamp on Lincoln's speech, too. A southern Indiana dialect would barb his tongue all his life.

Like his neighbors, young Lincoln said "howdey" to visitors. He "sot" down and "stayed a spell." He came "outen" a cabin and "yearned" his wages and "made a heap." He "cum" from "whar" he had been. He was "hornswoggled" into doing something against his better judgment. He "keered" for his friends and "heered" the latest news. He pointed to "yonder" stream and addressed the head of a committee as "Mr. Cheermun." And he got an "eddication" in log cabin schools and "larned" about adversity, self reliance and the necessity for mutual cooperation with his neighbors.[21]

Wrestling and struggling for knowledge were part of Lincoln's drive to master his rugged environment. He liked to exert his power over other people, both in wrestling holds and in words, as his cousin noted.

Sometimes, when he went to a log-house raising, corn shucking and suchlike things, he would say: "I don't want those fellows to work any more" and instantly he would commence his pranks, tricks, jokes, stories and sure enough all would stop, gather round Abe and listen, sometimes crying and sometimes bursting their sides with laughter.[22]

Animals were also a challenge.

Needing another ox, Tom Lincoln bought one from William Wood, an enterprising farmer who lived midway between Gentryville and Elizabeth, about a mile and a half north of the Lincoln farm. A night or two later the ox, named Buck, broke out and wandered off home and Tom sent Abe to bring the animal back. Abe found Buck contentedly grazing in a field. After helping to drive the ox into a barnlot, Mr. Wood offered a rope: "You can lead Buck with this." "No," said Abe, "I won't lead him. I'll ride that ox home

and make him pay for his smartness."

While Abe cut a gad, the entire Wood family came out to see the show. He leaped onto the ox's back and waved at Wood's attractive daughter, Elizabeth. Buck stood immovable. "Get out of here!" yelled Abe. Buck didn't move. Abe jammed his heels hard into Buck's flanks. Resenting that, Buck jumped high into the air and came down with a jolt on all fours. Around and around the barnlot the ox leaped and bawled, swayed, kicked, bucked, did everything an ox could do to throw off a rider. But Abe Lincoln stuck on tighter than a hungry tick, for Elizabeth Wood was watching him. Her father shouted, "Better get off and lead him! He'll break your neck against that fence!"

On and on went the struggle between Abe Lincoln and Buck. "Have the bars down 'gin we get around again!" finally yelled Abe.

Wood ran to the bars, but before he could lay them down Buck made another circuit and headed straight for him. Frantically, Wood jumped aside. The ox leaped the bars and headed down the road, Lincoln sticking on. They covered the first mile in no time. Buck slowed to a walk. Then Abe laid it on heavy with the gad. Panting, his tail drooping, the ox went into a jog trot. As they entered the Lincoln barnyard, Abe grinned at Tom and patted Buck: "I gentled him, Pap."[23]

In 1826, when Lincoln was seventeen, he got a job operating a ferry at the mouth of Anderson Creek, a half mile below present-day Troy, Indiana. Kentucky, with its numerous slave plantations, was visible across the river. Often the slaves could be heard singing as they toiled in the fields. The ferryman's job exposed Lincoln to another main American highway, the Mississippi and Ohio river valleys, along which flowed half the commerce of the young nation. He saw immense flatboats and keelboats, sometimes with white crews, sometimes manned by black slaves, churning steamboats loaded with well-dressed passengers as well as goods. He heard the names of the great river towns, Cincinnati, Natchez, Memphis, New Orleans, Pittsburgh and St. Louis. He got the feel of America's tremendous size and vitality.

In 1828 Lincoln took the first of his two flatboat voyages to New Orleans. He sailed with Allen Gentry, the son of a Pigeon Creek neighbor.

An Englishman named John Baillie went down the Ohio and the Mississippi in 1828 only a few months before Lincoln. In his diary he described huge flocks of wild turkeys on the shore. He marveled at the "fierce and tempestuous current" of the Mississippi and groaned over whole days when "we had no view save the interminable forest." They lived on wild turkeys, which Baillie pronounced "the finest flavored birds I ever tasted." River water was all that was available for drinking. Lower down, he was impressed by the great cottonwood and sugar trees. Soon he was marveling at the banks lined with cypress trees, covered with Spanish moss "in dark and somber festoons, adding a funereal aspect to the dreary view; quite in character with the deadly malignity of the climate."[24]

New Orleans, with its 50,000 people and its teeming wharves, where as many as 1,500 flatboats tied up, as well as dozens of river steamboats and oceangoing vessels from around the world, was the first great city Lincoln had ever seen. The elegant houses, with their painted sides and elaborate iron grillwork on their porches, the imposing Cathedral of St. Louis overlooking the Place d'Armes, the streets teeming with blacks, quadroons, Indians, and foreigners, were a startling contrast to the rude log homes and churches of southern Indiana. Among its other attractions, New Orleans had several thriving theaters. At one, a popular Shakespearean actor was playing Richard III. His name was Junius Brutus Booth. Ten years later he became the father of John Wilkes Booth.

Lincoln had seen occasional slaves sold in Kentucky and even in southern Indiana. But New Orleans was his first encounter with the slave market, where blacks were sold like cattle. The New Orleans *Argus* for December 27, 1828, advertised "Virginia and North Carolina slaves for sale. 29 young Virginia slaves of both sexes to be sold cheap for cash. 43 Virginia slaves, women, men, girls, and boys, may be bartered for sugar or to be sold on a liberal credit say for one or two years. 24 North Carolina slaves of both sexes to be sold cheap for cash or on a short credit. North Carolina slaves being 5 large robust men and four women and girls in which a bargain will be offered. John Clay, 44 Gravier St."[25]

One morning in their rambles they passed a slave auction. A vigorous and comely mulatto girl was being sold. She underwent a thorough examination at the hands of the bidders. They pinched her flesh and made her trot up and down the room like a horse, to show how she moved, and in order, as the auctioneer said, that the bidders might "satisfy themselves" whether the article they were offering to buy was sound or not. The whole thing was so revolting that Lincoln moved away from the scene with a deep feeling of "unconquerable hate."[26]

When Lincoln reached twenty-one, his father, beguiled by tales of richer soil in Illinois, decided to move there. Lincoln felt obligated to help him. It was an exhausting journey through spring mud, across swollen creeks and rivers. Dennis Hanks described it many years later.

It tuk us two weeks to get thar, raftin' over the Wabash, cuttin' our way through the woods, fordin' rivers, pryin' wagons and steers out o' sloughs with fence rails, an' makin' camp. Abe cracked a joke every time he cracked a whip, an' he found a way out o' every tight place while the rest of us was standin' round scratchin' our fool heads. I reckon Abe an' Aunty Sairy [Sarah] run that movin', an' good thing they did, or it'd ben run into a swamp and sucked under.[27]

Illinois in 1830 was almost as primitive as Indiana when the Lincolns had arrived there in 1816. There were no roads, only trails. There was an even more formidable natural challenge—the prairies.

The vast prairies were regarded as unfit to till, for they were under water a good part of the year. The grass which covered them was like a jungle, growing six to eight feet high, while the sod was so tough no plow then known could cut it. Yet these plains were uniquely beautiful. Those who remember them tell you of acres upon acres of blue iris, so thick that one could scarcely pass through it—of strawberries so many and so big that the legs of the horses would be stained red to the knees.[28]

After a year in Macon County, during which Lincoln worked at odd jobs, often involving the use of an ax, his parents decided to move to Coles County, settling within the boundaries of the present township of Pleasant Groves. Lincoln meanwhile took his second flatboat voyage down the Mississippi. On his return to Coles County, he was challenged by the local wrestling champion, huge Daniel Needham, to decide who was "the best man in the country."

Abe valued his popularity among "the boys" too highly to decline it and met him by public appointment in the "greenwood" at Wabash Point, where he threw him twice with so much ease that Needham's pride was hurt more than his body.

"Lincoln," said he, "you have thrown me twice, but you can't whip me" [in a prizefight].

"Needham," replied Abe, "are you satisfied that I can throw you? If you are not, and must be convinced through a threshing, I will do that too, for your sake."

Needham concluded that a bloody nose and a black eye would be the reverse of soothing to his feelings and surrendered the field."[29]

24

New Orleans levee scene, one of the earliest photographs of the city, taken between 1855 and 1860. Reportedly it was taken from the incomplete Custom House by General Beauregard. (Photo: The Historic New Orleans Collection)

On his own now, with no further obligations to his parents, Lincoln drifted into the village of New Salem on the Sangamon River, twenty miles northwest of Springfield. Here is how a contemporary described it.

New Salem was in many ways an America in miniature. It had people from New Hampshire, Vermont, New York, Pennsylvania, North Carolina, Tennessee, Kentucky and Virginia. They were men and women of more than usually strong individuality. Once a lawyer asked one of them what the "principal citizens" thought of a certain subject. He was told: "New Salem neighborhood has no 'principal citizens.' Every man there is a principal citizen."[30]

New Salem had a surprising number of well-educated residents, including two doctors. But there was also a contingent of what one writer charitably described as "the skirmish line on the borders of civilization." They were called The Clary's Grove boys because many of them came from a settlement of that name about five miles from New Salem. Their leader was Jack Armstrong.

Although there never was under the sun a more generous parcel of ruffians than those over whom Jack held sway, a stranger's introduction to them was likely to be most unpleasant. . . . They first bantered the gentleman to run a foot-race, jump, or wrestle; and if none of these propositions seemed agreeable to him they would request what he would do in case another gentleman should pull his nose or squirt tobacco juice in his face. If he did not seem entirely decided in his views as to what should properly be done in such a contingency, perhaps he would be nailed in a hogshead and rolled down New Salem Hill; perhaps his ideas would be brightened by a ducking in the Sangamon. If, however, the stranger consented to tussle with one of his persecutors, and proved to be a man of mettle, he would be promptly received into "good society" and would never have better friends on earth.[31]

Lincoln took on the Clary's Grove champion, Jack Armstrong, and wrestled him to a draw. When his friends cried foul and tried to start a riot, Lincoln offered to fight the whole crowd. But Jack Armstrong declared Lincoln

Come of age and on his own, Lincoln drifted into the village of New Salem, on the Sangamon River, northwest of Springfield, Illinois. "Every man there is a principal citizen," said one contemporary. (Photo: Arthur Shay)

"the best fellow that ever broke into the settlement," and thenceforth the two reigned "like friendly Caesars over the toughs and bullies of New Salem."[32]

During his six years in New Salem, Lincoln sought the help of the educated citizens to repair a deficiency that tormented him, his lack of education. Seeking a livelihood, he bought a partnership in a store, meanwhile keeping up his studies in his spare time. Lincoln was a failure as a storekeeper partly because he chose an alcoholic partner, partly because he had little business sense. When it came to wrestling, however, he had no self-doubts—and his irrepressible humor often came into play.

Once Lincoln was second in a bloody fight in which his man was whipped. While the contestants were washing themselves in the river, the second of the victor, a small man, somewhat the worse for drink, cried, "Abe, my man licked yours and I can lick you." Lincoln gravely accepted the challenge provided his opponent would chalk his outline on Lincoln and agree not to hit outside the lines.[33]

His local popularity inspired Lincoln to run for the Illinois legislature. His continuing feelings of inferiority were poignantly visible in his election statement, which he wrote and had printed in Springfield's *Sangamo Journal.*

Every man is said to have his peculiar ambition. Whether it be true or not, I can say for one that I have no other so great as that of being truly esteemed of my fellow men, by rendering myself worthy of their esteem. How far I shall succeed in gratifying this ambition, is yet to be developed. I am young and unknown to many of you. I was born and have ever remained in the most humble walks of life. I have no wealthy or popular relations to recommend me. My case is thrown exclusively upon the independent voters of this country, and if elected they will have conferred a favor upon me, for which I shall be unremitting in my labors to compensate. But if the good people in their wisdom shall see fit to keep me in the background, I have been too familiar with disappointments to be very much chagrined. Your friend and fellow-citizen.

New Salem, March 9, 1832.

A. Lincoln[34]

The tavern in New Salem, where Lincoln lived. During his six years in New Salem, Lincoln sought the help of the educated citizens to repair a deficiency that tormented him, his lack of education. (Photo: Arthur Shay)

Events now drew Lincoln in another direction. The Sac Indian chief Black Hawk went on the war path with some 500 warriors. Illinois called out its militia, and in the style of the day Lincoln's friends elected him captain of their company. He and his fellow recruits pursued the elusive red men up the Rock River into the swamps around Wisconsin's Lake Koshkonong. Their route is now marked by a number of monuments, including a heroic statue of Black Hawk on the Rock River bluffs, and "Lincoln's Tree," where legend has it that Captain Lincoln was nearly eaten alive by mosquitoes. The site where he and his men were mustered into U.S. service is known today as Lincoln Camp. It is just west of the town of Milan, on the south bank of the Rock River.[35]

Lincoln never led his men in battle, but he did arrive at a battlefield in time to bury five men killed in a skirmish. He later described it in a way that fixes it both in the mind and in the midwestern landscape.

The red light of the morning sun was streaming upon them as they lay heads towards us on the ground, and every man had a round red spot on the top of his head about as big as a dollar where the redskins had taken his scalp. It was frightful, but it was grotesque; and the red sunlight seemed to paint everything all over.[36]

Lincoln lost his first election, although he got 277 of the 284 votes cast in his district, where everyone knew him. He tried working as New Salem's postmaster, but the town was too small to make the job profitable. With a $1,100 debt from the failure of his store to pay off ("The National Debt," he sometimes called it) he gave himself a crash course in surveying. He was an instant success. Even in this largely mathematical business, Lincoln revealed his innate kindness.

In *Mitch Miller,* which is set in Petersburg, the town that eventually absorbed New Salem, one of Edgar Lee Masters' characters tells a story in local dialect which has been confirmed by the original Lincoln survey, still in the town records.

Look at this house partly in the street and look at the street how it jigs. Well, Linkern did that. You see he surveyed this whole town of Petersburg. But as to this, this is how it happened. You see it was

In the Black Hawk Indian War Illinois called out its militia and Lincoln's friends elected him captain of their company. He and his fellow recruits pursued the elusive red men into Wisconsin and countryside filled with beautiful vistas and mosquitos of legendary ferocity. (Photo: Arthur Shay)

after the Black Hawk War in '36 and when Linkern came here to survey, he found that Jemina Elmore, which was a widow of Linkern's friend in the war, had a piece of land, and had built a house on it and was livin' here with her children. And Linkern saw if the street run straight north and south, a part of her house would be in the street. So to save Jemina's house, he set his compass to make the line run a little furder south. And so this is how the line got skewed and leans this strip kind of irregular clear through the town north and south. This is what I call makin' a mistake that is all right, bein' good and bad at the same time.[37]

Encouraged by the money he was making as a surveyor, Lincoln began thinking of an even larger ambition, to become a lawyer. But before he could progress beyond a painful first reading of Blackstone, he fell in love. Her name was Ann Rutledge; she was nineteen and auburn-haired. Lincoln boarded at her father's tavern. Compared to Lincoln, the Rutledges were aristocrats, descended from a South Carolina signer of the Declaration of Independence. There were other problems. Ann was engaged to another man, a dubious character, who, it turned out, traveled under an assumed name, went east on supposedly family business, and vanished from her life. After much delay, Ann accepted Lincoln's proposal, and they became engaged. They planned to wait a year, while Ann studied at a female academy in Jacksonville and Lincoln continued his legal studies. But in the summer of 1835 Ann succumbed to a siege of the malarial fever which killed so many pioneers.

Lincoln was distraught. For days he could not eat or sleep. His face was haggard with mental agony. Ann's brother said: "The effect upon Mr. Lincoln's mind was terrible. He became plunged in despair, and many of his friends feared that reason would desert her throne." He complained that he could not bear the thought of "the snow and rain falling on her grave," and on stormy, gloomy days was closely watched for fear he would take his own life.[38]

Around this time, while he was grieving for Ann Rutledge, Lincoln encountered a poem, "Immortality," which he memorized and recited dozens of times for friends throughout his life. The theme is struck in the opening stanza:

Oh! Why should the spirit of mortal be proud?
Like a swift fleeting meteor, a fast flying cloud
A flash of the lightning, a break of the wave
He passeth from life to rest in his grave.

One stanza must have seemed especially apropos to the griefstricken lover.

The maid on whose cheek, on whose brow, in whose eye,
Shone beauty and pleasure,—her triumphs are bye;
And the memory of those who loved her and praised,
Are alike from the minds of the living erased.[39]

A Greek poet tells us that grief walks the earth and sits at the feet of each by turns. She certainly lingered along the path of Abraham Lincoln's life, casting her shadows about him with unusual persistency. It was a strange sad school through which he passed during all his years.[40]

During his courtship of Ann, Lincoln had made another run for the Illinois legislature. This time he won. Recovering from his grief, he made steady progress in his study of the law. Friends he met in the legislature encouraged him, lent him books, and advised him to leave New Salem, which was too small to support a lawyer, and move to the new state capital, Springfield. In 1837 he accepted the offer of a partnership from John T. Stuart, a prominent lawyer who had been impressed by Lincoln's speeches and political shrewdness in the legislature. On April 12, 1837, the following notice appeared in the *Sangamo Journal*:

J. T. STUART AND A. LINCOLN
Attorneys and counsellors at Law, will practice conjointly in the courts of this judicial circuit. Office No 4 Hoffman's Row, upstairs.[41]

CHAPTER TWO

Lincoln's journey to greatness had begun. He also began another

33

kind of journey, across the prairies of Illinois to the fifteen county seats of the Eighth Judicial Circuit. The original circuit covered an area 120 miles long and about 85 miles wide. Its zigzag boundaries encompassed some 10,000 square miles, about a quarter of Illinois. The Daughters of the American Revolution have placed granite slabs along the route, which now passes through prosperous farm country. In each of the county seats the DAR has placed bronze tablets designed by Henry Bacon, who created the Lincoln Memorial. From Springfield to Tremont to Pekin to Metamora to Bloomington to Mount Pulaski (whose original red brick courthouse still stands) to Clinton to Monticello to Urbana to Danville to Paris to Shelbyville (the longest haul on the circuit, 55 miles) to Sullivan to Decatur and finally to Taylorville, the lawyers rode in search of business. At its greatest length (the legislature made frequent alterations), it took a lawyer twelve weeks to cover the 400-mile route. It was rugged traveling, over roads frequently swamped by spring rain or melting snow, across flooded streams.

Lincoln never complained about the poor food and atrocious accommodations at the prairie hotels and taverns. A fellow lawyer, Gibson W. Harris, recalled in later years some details of the Eighth Circuit's accommodations.

The taverns, invariably so called, were almost always cheerless and uncomfortable. . . . The "transient" of those days could not be sure of finding his hostelry so much as waterproof; more than once I have slept with tiny eddies of snow drifting in upon my bed. The furniture in the great chamber rarely comprised more than the bedstead, one or two split-bottom chairs, and possibly a spittoon. The bedding was usually abundant, perchance the bedbugs superabundant. The guests performed their ablutions in a tin basin on the back porch, or on a bench out by the wall in the yard, using soft soap, if any soap at all, and wiping on a crash towel that late risers were sure to find too wet for effective service. I distinctly remember washing at the well one morning when the thermometer was thirty degrees below zero, the water freezing on the basin-side as it dropped from my hands. It was either this or postponing the rite to another day.[42]

34

Usually the lawyers moved in a group of perhaps twenty-five, including David Davis, the portly circuit court judge. They were a gregarious, often hilarious troupe, with Lincoln the acknowledged leader in jokes, pranks, and tall stories. Thomas W. S. Kidd, a newspaper editor who doubled as a court official in Springfield, recalled one of Lincoln's better tricks.

Heavy rains having fallen some days before, they [Judge Davis and the circuit's lawyers] were led to believe that Salt Creek had overflowed its banks and formed a more direct channel, and they would either have to travel many miles around or swim the supposed creek.

Lincoln saw that it was only a swale, and the water could be but a few inches in depth at most. He suggested that it was better to swim than to travel around, and to prepare for any emergency by undressing to insure their being dry on the other side. They at once took with the suggestion, dismounted, divested themselves of their clothes, and securing them knapsack-like on their backs, after remounting, they proceeded to cross, Lincoln leading off. What a picture was there presented for the pencil of an artist. Talent that has since become world-known for depth and brilliancy! Intellects that have made reputations as proud for Illinois and the Union as for themselves! Nothing could be heard but the gentle voices endeavoring to persuade their horses on to a swim, holding with steady hand the rein, and with faces the very index of anxious expectancy, watching every step of the faithful animals until the other side of the supposed new channel was reached. Then a vacant look of astonishment at each other revealed that in no place had the water covered the fetlocks of their horses. Mr. Lincoln broke forth in one of his loudest bursts of laughter, and said: "Judge, I don't think a bridge across that stream would seriously interfere with navigation."[43]

Although Lincoln did not drink, he often stood at the bar with his fellow lawyers. In Mount Pulaski, on one of these occasions, early in his legal career, he was with Stephen A. Douglas, not yet his great Democratic rival, several other lawyers, and a juror named James

Robinson, who was nicknamed Know-All Robinson. A discussion arose about paying for a round of drinks. Know-All protested he had paid for the previous round. Lincoln's friend Isaac Arnold tells the rest of the story.

Abe said: "We are no dead beats, but we are all broke. You set them up until some of us have a trial and we get some money and we will even up."

Know-All said: "No; I have a proposition. Every man who asks a question he can't answer himself shall set them up," and they all accepted.

Abe said: "What is the reason there is no dirt at the mouth of those ground squirrels' dens?"

They all pleaded ignorance and couldn't tell and Abe would have to tell, and they seemed to think they had Abe for the drinks. Abe said: "The reason is that they begin to dig at the bottom."

Know-All put in and said: "Abe, how do they get to the bottom to commence?" and Abe said: "Know-All, that is your question, you answer it!"[44]

William Herndon, who later became Lincoln's law partner, recalled some late-evening antics on the circuit.

I was told that I would find Mr. Lincoln in Judge Davis's room. I climbed the unbanistered stairway, and to my timid knock two voices responded almost simultaneously: "Come in!"

Imagine my surprise, when the door opened, to find two men undressed, or rather dressed for bed, engaged in a lively battle with pillows, flinging them at each other's head; one, a low, heavy-set man, who, leaning against the bed and puffing like a lizard, answered to the description of Judge Davis; the other, a man of tremendous stature, looking as if he were at least seven feet tall, was incased in a long garment, yellow as saffron, which reached to his heels, and from beneath which protruded two of the largest feet that, up to that time, it had ever been my privilege to see. I cannot fully describe my sensations as this apparition, with the modest announcement, "My name is Lincoln, sir," strode across the room, and grasped my hand.[45]

*The Circuit Court in Mount Pulaski.
Lincoln and a group of about twenty-five
lawyers and the circuit court judge
rode by horse across the prairies
of Illinois to the fifteen county seats of
the Eighth Judicial Circuit.
(Photo: Arthur Shay)*

*As a trial lawyer Lincoln
had few peers in his time.
In Beardstown he tried his most
famous case, his defense
of Duff Armstrong against a
charge of murder. Shown here
is the jail cell where
Lincoln visited Armstrong.
(Photo: Arthur Shay)*

A fellow lawyer, Daniel Voorhees (afterward senator from Indiana), complaining of a decision rendered against them in a case in which they had appeared as co-counsel, asked Lincoln "What can we do?" "Well," said Lincoln, "we can go over to the tavern and, just among ourselves, cuss the judge to our hearts' content."[46]

Occasionally his fellow lawyers glimpsed the poverty and deprivation of Lincoln's boyhood.

One evening, Lincoln was missing immediately after supper; he had no place to go that we could think of—no friend to visit—no business to do—no client to attend to: and certainly no entertainment to go to: hence "Where is Lincoln?" was the question. I visited all the law offices and stores, but got no trace whatever: and at nine o'clock—an early hour for us—Davis and I went to bed, leaving the problem unsolved. Now, Lincoln had a furtive way of stealing in on one, unheard, unperceived and unawares: and on this occasion, after we had lain for a short time, our door latch was noiselessly raised—the door opened, and the tall form of Abraham Lincoln glided in. "Why Lincoln, where *have* you been?" exclaimed the Judge. "I was in hopes you fellers would be asleep," replied he: "Well, I have been to a little show up at the Academy": and he sat before the fire, and narrated all the sights of that most primitive of country shows, given chiefly to school children—a magic lantern, electrical machine, etc. I told him I had seen all these sights at school. "Yes," said he, sadly, "I now have an advantage over you in, for the first time in my life, seeing these things which are of course common to those who had a chance at an education when they were young."[47]

One day in Decatur, Lincoln stopped in front of the courthouse. "Here on this spot," he said, "I made my first halt in Illinois. Here I stood and there our wagon stood, with all that we owned in the world."[48]

In spite of the poverty of his youth, Lincoln was relatively indifferent to getting rich. A younger lawyer, Ward Hill Lamon, recalled an encounter with this Lincoln attitude.

One of the first things I learned after getting under way as a lawyer was to charge well for legal services—a branch of the practice that Mr. Lincoln could never learn. He at length left that department entirely to me. A gentleman named Scott had a demented sister who possessed property to the amount of $10,000, mostly in cash. A conservator, as he was called, had been appointed to take charge of the estate and we were employed to resist a motion to remove him. The case was tried inside of twenty minutes; our success was complete. Scott cheerfully paid over the fee to me. Mr. Lincoln asked, "What did you charge that man?" I told him $250. "Lamon, that is all wrong," he said. "Give him back at least half of it."

I protested that the fee was fixed in advance; that Scott was perfectly satisfied. "But I am not satisfied," Lincoln said. "Return half the money at least, or I will not receive one cent of it for my share."

Judge David Davis called Lincoln to him and in rasping tones that could be heard all over the courtroom said: "Lincoln, you are impoverishing this bar by your picayune charges of fees. You are

now almost as poor as Lazarus and if you don't make people pay you more for your services you will die as poor as Job's turkey."

Lincoln was immovable. "That money," he said, "comes out of the pocket of a poor demented girl and I would rather starve than swindle her."[49]

As a trial lawyer Lincoln had few peers in his time. One reason is visible in this recollection of John T. Birch, a young man whom Lincoln examined for admission to the bar.

His first question was, "What books have you read?" When I told him, he said, "Well, that is more than I had read before I was admitted to practice." Then he paused long enough to tell a story of something that befell him in a county in Southern Illinois where he once tried a case in which he was pitted against a college-bred lawyer who apparently had studied all the books and was very proud of his accomplishment. The court and all the lawyers were profoundly impressed by the man's wonderful store of learning, but it was all lost on the jury, "And they," said

Lincoln, laughingly, "were the fellows I was aiming at."[50]

In Metamora, Illinois, Lincoln was hired to defend Melissa Goings, aged seventy, who had killed her seventy-seven-year-old husband in a drunken quarrel. No one had any enthusiasm for prosecuting the case. On the day of the trial, Lincoln asked permission to consult privately with his client. It was granted. He apparently left her in the room where they met, on the lower floor of the Metamora courthouse. When she was called to trial, the agitated bailiff, Robert T. Cassell, reported Melissa had vanished.

"Confound you, Abe, you have run her off," Cassell said.

"Oh, no, Bob," replied Lincoln. "I didn't run her off. She wanted to know where she could get a good drink of water, and I told her there was mighty good water in Tennessee."

No one pursued Melissa. Two years later the case was dropped.[51]

When his tour of the circuit brought him to Charleston, county seat of Coles County, Lincoln almost always visited his father and stepmother in nearby Goosenest Prairie.

We may picture Abraham in a hired two-horse buggy making the seven mile drive to Goosenest Prairie, the floor at his feet piled with groceries—a sack of flour, a bag of sugar, a bag of coffee beans, and probably a twist of tobacco for Thomas and a few bags of rock candy for the Johnston children, who with their parents lived with Thomas and Sarah. It will not stretch the imagination to include a bolt of cloth for his stepmother, and even a bright shawl or a warm "comforter" for the old lady. "Land sakes, Abe," she would say with pretended dismay, "why did you bring me such fol-der-ols?"[52]

A recent student of Lincoln as a lawyer has linked his circuit journeys to his development as a man.

To one of his inbred melancholy, the pensive loneliness of prairie travel exercised a special fascination.... Riding often times past sundown, during nights in the late fall when the bright moonlight shone on a sea of untrodden snow, it was quiet, prairie quiet, with only an owl or a fox speaking or a distant dog. In those days and nights of circuit travel, when the scene breathed the very essence of solitude, Lincoln became a man of deep cogitation.[53]

Many years ago, poet James Russell Lowell saw a similar Lincoln kinship with the prairies.

His was no lofty mountain-peak of mind,
Thrusting to thin air o'er cloudy bars,
A sea-mark now, now lost in varpors blind;
Broad prairie rather, genial, level-lined,
Fruitful and friendly for all human kind.[54]

Six gentlemen, I being one, were riding along a country road. We were strung along the road two and two together. We were passing through a thicket of wild plum and crabapple trees. A violent windstorm had just occurred. There were two young birds by the roadside too young to fly. They had been blown from the nest by the storm. The old bird was fluttering about and wailing as a mother ever does for her babes. Lincoln stopped, hitched his horse, caught the birds, hunted the nest and placed them in it. The rest of us rode on to a creek, and while our horses were drinking Hardin rode up. "Where is Lincoln?" said one. "Oh, when I saw him last he had two little birds in his hand hunting for their nest." In perhaps an hour he came. They laughed at him. He said with much emphasis, "Gentlemen, you may laugh, but I could not have slept well tonight, if I had not saved those birds. Their cries would have rung in my ears."[55]

In Beardstown, Lincoln tried his most famous case, his defense of Duff Armstrong against a charge of murder. No case meant more to Lincoln on a personal level. Duff's father, Jack Armstrong, had been Lincoln's battling friend from New Salem days. His mother, Hannah, had been an openhanded hostess, feeding and fussing over Lincoln at a time when he had no home of his own. Jack had died shortly after Duff was indicted. Hannah appealed to Lincoln, by now one of the best-known attorneys in Illinois. He instantly put aside all other business to defend Duff without a fee.

The crucial witness in the case was a house painter named Charles Allen, who claimed that he had seen young Armstrong strike the victim, Metzker, with a slingshot. Although it was 11 P.M. when the fight between the two men erupted, and Allen was 150 feet away, Allen insisted he had seen it all by the light of a full moon. Allen's testimony had already sent another man, accused of the same crime, to prison. He seemed unassailable. Lincoln rose to cross-examine him.

Hooking his fingers under his gallus straps, which held up shapeless trousers, the cool, unruffled prairie lawyer took the chief prosecution witness over on cross-examination, pressing him with the most searching questions, asked with seeming casualness. He adroitly led him to commit himself irretrievably to the statement, repeated "a dozen or more times," that he could not be mistaken about what he had seen, because the moon was shining brightly at the time. Suddenly, dramatically, Lincoln fell upon the witness, riddling his testimony by confronting him with an almanac for 1857 which showed that at the hour of the alleged fracas the moon was not in the position stated by Allen, but, rather, was low in the sky, within an hour of setting. One can see the witness twisting and wriggling through the ordeal, like a sailfish coming to gaff,

while the laboriously constructed case for the prosecution crumbled. As several jurymen later stated, "The almanac floored the witness."[56]

As the jury filed out to deliberate, Lincoln turned to Mrs. Armstrong and said, "Aunt Hannah, your son will be free before sundown." He was.

In Cincinnati, Lincoln had his most humiliating experience as a lawyer. He was retained by the J. H. Manny Company to defend it in a lawsuit with the McCormick Reaper interests over a supposed patent infringement on the famous reaping machine, which had already revolutionized farming by doing the work of ten strong men. Arriving in the city on September 19, 1855, Lincoln went to the Burnet House to confer with George Harding, a well-known patent lawyer from Philadelphia, and Edwin M. Stanton of Ohio, then considered one of the foremost trial lawyers in the nation. They were to be co-counsel. Stanton, arrogance personified, declared himself the chief counsel and looked down his nose at the rumpled prairie lawyer. Upon learning that Lincoln had been retained principally to make the closing arguments, Stanton flew into a rage and dismissed

Beardstown courtroom. No case meant more to Lincoln on a personal level than defending Duff Armstrong. His father, Jack, had been Lincoln's friend from New Salem days. His mother, Hannah, fed and fussed over Lincoln at a time when he had no home of his own. (Photo: Arthur Shay)

him scornfully as "that long-armed baboon." He informed the Manny Company that "if that giraffe appears in the case, I will throw up my brief and leave." The Manny interests decided they had no choice. They reluctantly advised Lincoln that his services were no longer required.

Suppressing his disappointment, Lincoln stayed in Cincinnati for a week attending the trial and listening intently to Stanton's prodigious efforts in summation, which won the case. A glimpse of Lincoln's mortification is visible in his farewell to his landlady. "You have made my stay here most agreeable. I am a thousand times obliged to you," he said, "but in reply to your request for me to come again, I must say to you I never expect to be in Cincinnati again. I have nothing against the city, but things have happened here as to make it undesirable for me ever to return here."[57]

Four years later, Lincoln returned to Cincinnati as a presidential candidate.

On Rock Island in the Mississippi opposite Davenport, Iowa, lawyer Lincoln renewed his long friendship with the Father of Waters and incidentally won one of his most important cases. The railroad bridge at Rock Island was the first to span the Mississippi. On May 6, 1856, the steamboat *Effie Afton* was passing through the draw of the bridge when one of its side wheels struck a pier. The steamer caught fire and burned to the water's edge. The owners contended it was the bridge's fault—it was a menace to navigation. The case was a confrontation between the steamboat interests and the railroad interests for control of the commerce of the nation. If railroads could not span rivers with bridges, they would never be able to compete with the far-ranging steamboats. By painstaking investigation, including hours of consultation with pilots and rivermen, and more hours aboard a chartered steamboat going back and forth beneath the bridge, Lincoln was able to prove that the captain of the *Effie Afton* had been negligent, and the draw was no more menacing to navigation than a hundred other natural rips and eddies on the great river.[58]

No matter how successful he became, part of Lincoln remained the uneducated young man who had drifted into New Salem in 1831.

In 1853, Lincoln was retained by friends in Logan County to draw up the necessary papers for a new town, designed to become the county seat. Lincoln did so, and informed the incorporators that he needed a name for the town so he could submit the bill to the legislature. They decided to name it Lincoln. "You'd better not do that," Lincoln said. "Nothing named Lincoln has ever amounted to much."[59]

CHAPTER THREE

Not long after he became a lawyer, Lincoln took a side trip to Farmington, the Kentucky home of his closest friend, Joshua Speed. In a thank-you letter to Mary Speed, Joshua's sister, Lincoln said he was "living upon the remembrance of the delicious dishes of peaches and cream we used to have at your house." Mrs. Speed had given him an Oxford Bible, and Lincoln asked Mary to tell her mother that he intended to read it regularly. He then described his steamboat journey back to Illinois. Here the letter revealed his growing sensitivity to the great national problem—slavery. He obviously

detested it. But he had not yet decided what could be done about it.

We got aboard the steamboat *Lebanon* about twelve o'clock M. [sic] of the day we left, and reached St. Louis the next Monday at 8 P.M. . . . By the way, a fine example was presented on board the boat for contemplating the effect of condition upon human happiness. A gentleman had purchased twelve negroes in different parts of Kentucky, and was taking them to a farm in the South. They were chained six and six together. A small iron clevis was around the left wrist of each, and this was fastened to the main chain by a shorter one, at a convenient distance from the others, so that the negroes were strung together precisely like so many fish upon a trot-line. In this condition they were being separated forever from the scenes of their childhood, their friends, their fathers and mothers, and brothers and sisters, and many of them from their wives and children, and going into perpetual slavery, where the lash of the master is proverbially more ruthless and unrelenting than any other where; and yet amid all these distressing circumstances, as we would think them, they were the most cheerful and apparently happy creatures on board. One whose offense for which he had been sold was an over-fondness for his wife, played the fiddle almost continually, and the others danced, sang, cracked jokes, and played various games with cards from day to day. How true it is that "God tempers the wind to the shorn lamb," or in other words, that he renders the worst of human conditions tolerable, while he permits the best to be nothing better than tolerable.[60]

Lincoln did not spend all his days and nights on the Eighth Judicial Circuit. Springfield, the capital of Illinois and the seat of Sangamon County, was his home. Here he took one of the more momentous steps in his life, marrying high-spirited, aristocratic Mary Todd of Kentucky on November 4, 1842, after a stormy two-year courtship. At first they lived in the Globe Tavern, but they moved in 1844, after the birth of their son Robert, to a "little cottage" on the corner of Eighth and Jackson streets. It is the only house Lincoln ever owned. Here is a description of it, written in 1907 by Albert S. Edwards, the man who was its custodian for many years.

It is a plain, old-fashioned two-story wooden house of twelve rooms, fronting west on Eighth street, built in 1839 by Rev. Charles Dresser.

The frame work and all the floors of the old home are of oak; the laths of hickory, split out by hand; the doors, door frames, window frames and weatherboarding of black walnut. The nails, sparingly used in its construction, are all handmade. The most noticeable features of its construction from the builders' point of view, is the prodigal use of solid walnut and strict economy in the use of iron, wooden pegs being used wherever practicable in lieu of the customary nail. At the time of its construction it was one of the more pretentious residences of Springfield, located on the outskirts of the town.

At the time of its purchase by Mr. Lincoln it was painted white with green window shutters, after the fashion of the times, and but a story and a half in height. During one of Mr. Lincoln's campaigning tours in the "Forties," Mrs. Lincoln,

The only house Lincoln ever owned. A plain, old-fashioned two-story
wooden house of twelve rooms, fronting west on Eighth Street, built in 1839.
At the time of its construction it was one of the more pretentious residences
in Springfield, located on the outskirts of town (Photo: Arthur Shay)

while having a new roof put on the residence, took occasion to have it converted into a full two-story house, as it appears today. No changes have been made in the house since Mr. Lincoln left it, except the repairs rendered necessary by decay of the original material.[61]

Mary Lincoln had the traditional hot temper of the Kentucky belle. Lincoln usually did his best to avoid igniting it.

Lincoln was submissive to the woman in the home. It was her domain and she was its rightful ruler. A morning chore was to split the wood for the breakfast fire. Mrs. Lincoln, impatient to get the day's program started, often found it necessary to prod her liege lord to greater activity. From the kitchen door would issue the loud exclamation of "Fire! Fire! Fire!" The neighborhood understood its application and was not alarmed. Lincoln mildly replied, "Yes Mary, yes Mary."[62]

The one shade tree in front of the house was ordered cut down by Mrs. Lincoln to facilitate making some repairs.

The workmen hesitated and consulted Lincoln. "Have you seen Mrs. Lincoln?" he asked.

"Yes," said the man.

"Then in God's name cut it down clean to the roots," Lincoln responded.[63]

Lincoln's greatest weakness as a husband was an inability, amounting to indifference, to be on time for dinner. He was constantly tempted to stop at the barbershop or one of the stores along his route home to swap stories and talk politics with his Springfield neighbors. This glimpse of a dinnertime contretemps comes from Mary Lincoln's younger sister, who often visited the Lincolns in Springfield. The "Mr. Jay" she mentions was an invention of the Todd family's nurse, Mammy Sally, who maintained that jaybirds flew to hell each Friday night to tell Satan all the things children had done wrong in the preceding week.

One evening he was very late for supper and the impatient cook came several times to the door to see if he had come. Finally, two hours after the time set for the meal, in sauntered Brother Lincoln as innocent as a lamb of any infraction of domestic routine. Sister [Mrs. Lincoln] reminded him of the time and said: "I am afraid the chickens are burned to a crisp." Pointing his finger at his wife, with a quizzical smile Brother Lincoln said: "Nem mine. Mr. Jay's gwine tell ole man Satan that Mary sets her hungry husband down to burned up vittals just caze he's two minutes late." "Two minutes!" we cried in unison. "Two hours you mean." "Nem mine," said Brother Lincoln, "just bring on the cinders and see how quickly dey'll disappear."[64]

Another son, named Edward Baker, after one of Lincoln's closest lawyer friends, was born to the Lincolns in 1846. A few years later, a Springfield neighbor recalled the following encounter with Lincoln and the boys, near their home.

The father's arm was above his head and his hand closed. With the other hand he was restraining the boisterous struggles of both boys, who were trying to mount up to their father's shoulders and grasp what he held above his head. Diller said he was so surprised he exclaimed:

"Why, Mr. Lincoln, what is the matter with the boys?" Lincoln calmly replied. "Only what is the matter with all the rest of the world. I have three English walnuts and each boy wants two!"[65]

CHAPTER FOUR

One reason Lincoln never missed a swing around the Eighth Judicial Circuit twice a year was his "peculiar ambition"—to win high political office. The circuit gave him a priceless opportunity to see and be seen by thousands of people who often crowded the courtrooms to watch trials in progress. It also enabled him to mingle with his fellow lawyers, traditionally America's political leaders. But he refused to join the Democrats, by far the majority party in Illinois, because of their stated indifference to slavery. Lincoln joined the Whigs, their chief national opponents. In the East, the Whigs tended to be the better educated, more dignified class. In the West, they had to be as rough-and-tumble as their Democratic opponents. Lincoln was more than equal to this challenge.

Overleaf:. *The Springfield house; sitting room. (Photo: Arthur Shay)*

Colonel "Dick" Taylor, one of Lincoln's earlier Democratic political opponents, was wont to denounce the aristocratic proclivities of the Whigs and to extol the Spartan simplicity of himself and his Democratic confreres. One day, when he was expatiating in his usual style, Lincoln slipped up to his side, caught hold of the bottom of his vest and suddenly pulled it open, revealing to the astonished crowd a ruffled shirtfront adorned with a massive gold watch-chain, seals and other jewelry. The exponent of Democratic simplicity was dumfounded, while the audience roared with laughter.[66]

In 1844, Usher Lindner was speaking at the State House in Springfield on behalf of Henry Clay, who was running for president. "Some ruffian in the galleries," recalled one witness, flung at him "a gross personal insult, accompanied by a threat." Both Lincoln and Edward D. Baker jumped up on the platform and stood beside Lindner while he finished his speech. They then each took one of Lindner's arms and walked with him from the State House.

"Lindner, we both think we can do a little fighting," Lincoln said. "So we want you to walk between us until we get you to your hotel. Your quarrel is our quarrel and that of the great Whig party of the nation and your speech is the greatest one that has been made by any of us, for which we wish to honor, love and defend you."[67]

Only once did Lincoln use his skill as a mimic to discredit a political rival. Jesse B. Thomas, a leading Illinois Democrat, made the mistake of ridiculing Lincoln in a speech at the court house in Springfield. Lincoln hurried to the meeting and demanded a chance to reply. He imitated Thomas in gesture and voice, at times caricaturing his walk and the very motion of his body. Thomas, like everybody else, had some peculiarities of expression and gesture and these Lincoln succeeded in rendering ludicrous. Thomas was obliged to sit near by and endure the pain of this unique ordeal. He was so wrought up that he actually gave way to tears. For years afterwards it was called the "skinning" of Thomas. The next day, Lincoln felt he had gone too far, hunted up Thomas and made ample apology.[68]

Stump speaking sometimes revealed other, more unique sides of Lincoln's personality.

One day in Petersburg, while on the circuit, some of Lincoln's former New Salem friends called for a speech during the court's noon recess. Lincoln had been speaking only a few minutes when James Pantier arrived and pushed his way through the crowd to the edge of the platform. He was an old pioneer, who had worked as a hunter, trapper, faith doctor, saw-mill owner and farmer. He wore a mixture of frontier buckskin and home-woven clothes, and a brimless hat sat on the back of his head.

"Howdy Abe," he said. "Howdy Abe." When Lincoln did not hear him he said it a third time. "Howdy Abe!"

"Why how are you Uncle Jimmy?" Lincoln said. Leaning down, he shook hands and then, still holding the old man's hand, he led him along the front of the platform and up the steps, where he gave him a seat between two of the most dignified and aristocratic members of the Illinois bar. Lincoln returned to the front of the platform and resumed his speech.

In a few minutes, Uncle Jimmy grew restless. He had apparently forgotten something. Suddenly he remembered it. "Abe," he said. "Abe! I forgot to ax you about how Mary and the babies were."

Lincoln turned and in a low voice replied, "All well when I left them at Springfield yesterday morning, Uncle Jimmy."

Lincoln resumed his speech without the slightest trace of embarrassment or impatience. There was in Lincoln's conduct toward others, then and always, that which transcended manners.[69]

In 1846 Lincoln thought he was taking a long stride toward his "peculiar ambition" by winning election to Congress on the Whig ticket. He performed ably in Washington, attracting the attention of the Whig national leadership by his sarcastic attacks on President James Polk for rushing the United States into war with Mexico. Here are a few glimpses of Congressman Lincoln.

As to speech making, by way of getting the hang of the House, I made a little speech two or three days ago on a post office question of no general interest. I find speaking here and elsewhere about the same thing. I was about as badly scared, and no worse, as I am when I speak in court.[70]

Lincoln was convinced that the war with Mexico was instigated by the Americans who had invaded territory legally belonging to Mexico. He had some very lively correspondence with his constituents about it. He wrote the following letter to a minister, the Reverend J. M. Peck.

Possibly you consider these acts [of aggression by Americans] too small for notice. Would you venture to so consider them had they been committed by any nation on earth against the humblest of our people? I know you would not. Then I ask, is the precept, "Whatsoever ye would that men should do to you, do you even so to them," obsolete?[71]

In one speech Lincoln took a satiric swipe at

President Polk's argument that federally financed internal improvements were bad because their benefits were unequally distributed to all the states.

There are few stronger cases in this world of inequality than the presidency itself. An honest laborer digs coal at about seventy cents a day while the president digs abstractions at about seventy dollars a day.[72]

A fellow legislator E. B. Washburne, gives us this glimpse of Congressman Lincoln in Washington, D.C.

Mr. Lincoln came to the library of the Supreme Court one day for the purpose of procuring some law books which he wanted to take to his room for examination. Getting together all the books he wanted, he placed them in a pile on a table. Taking a large bandana handkerchief from his pocket, he tied them up, and putting a stick which he had brought with him through a knot he had made in the handkerchief, adjusting the package of books to his stick, he shouldered it, and marched off from the library to his room. In a few days he returned the books in the same way.[73]

Lincoln always disliked all forms of pretension. He wrote to his wife from Washington.

Suppose you do not prefix the "Hon" to the address on your letters to me any more. I like the letters very much, but I would rather they should not have that upon them. It is not necessary, as I suppose you have thought, to have them to come free.[74]

Asked to supply a sketch of his life for the *Dictionary of Congress,* Lincoln chose to put on record the barest essentials.

Born, February 12, 1809, in Hardin
   County, Kentucky.
Education defective.
Profession, a lawyer.
Have been a captain of volunteers in Black
   Hawk War.
Postmaster at a very small office.
Four times a member of the Illinois legis-
   lature, and was a member of the lower

house of Congress.

          A. Lincoln.[75]

In 1847 a Boston reporter, J. H. Buckingham, toured Illinois. During one stagecoach ride, he found himself in the company of two congressmen. The Whig was Lincoln. He was the only Whig congressman from Illinois. Locofoco was a nickname for the radical wing of the Democratic Party.

We had two members of Congress from the state of Illinois, one Whig and one Locofoco, and persons of other professions. . . . We started in a grumbling humor, but our Whig congressman was determined to be good natured, and to keep all the rest so if he could; he told stories, and badgered his opponent, who it appeared was an old personal friend, until we all laughed, in spite of the dismal circumstances in which we were placed. The character of the Western people is in every respect different from ours. . . .

We were [soon] in the district represented by our Whig Congressman, and he knew, or appeared to know, every body we met, the name of the tenant of every farmhouse, and the owner of every plot of ground. Such a shaking of hands—such a how-d'ye-do—such a greeting of different kinds . . . was never seen before; . . . and he had a kind word, a smile and a bow for every body on the road, even to the horses, and the cattle, and the swine.[76]

On one of his trips to Washington, Congressman Lincoln made a detour to visit his wife's family in Lexington, Kentucky. They went by stagecoach to St. Louis, Missouri. From there they took a steamboat down the Mississippi to Cairo, where the Ohio River joins the Father of Waters. Through that turbulent swirl they steamed up the Ohio and then up the Kentucky River to Frankfort, where they took a train that puffed up winding grades to Lexington, in the heart of Kentucky's blue grass country. The elegant town, with its finely painted stores, its public square lined with substantial brick houses, was known as the Athens of the West. Mary Lincoln's half sister, who was nine at the time, recalled the Lincolns' arrival.

The white family stood near the front door with welcoming arms and, in true patriarchal style, our colored contingent filled the rear of the hall to shake hands with the long-absent one and "make a'miration" over the babies. Mary came in first with little Eddie, the baby, in her arms. To my mind she was lovely; clear, sparkling blue eyes, lovely smooth white skin with a faint, wild rose color in her cheeks, and glossy light-brown hair, which fell in soft short curls behind each ear. She was then about twenty-nine years of age.

Mr. Lincoln followed her into the hall with his little son, Robert Todd, in his arms. He put the little fellow on the floor, and as he arose, I remember thinking of "Jack and the Bean Stalk," and feared he might be the hungry giant of the story—he was so tall and looked so big with a long, full, black cloak over his shoulders, and he wore a fur cap with ear straps which allowed but little of his face to be seen. Expecting to hear the "fe, fi, fo, fum," I shrank closer to my mother, and tried to hide behind her voluminous skirts. After shaking hands with all the grown-ups, he turned and, lifting me in his arms, said, "So this is Little Sister." His voice and smile banished my fear of the giant.[77]

In 1848 Lincoln stumped in Massachusetts for the national Whig ticket. At the party's state convention in Worcester, he was diffident about speaking to people "this side of the mountains," people who were "instructed and wise." Nevertheless, his relaxed western style made an impression on audiences used to more formal oratory. George Monroe, a young Whig, recalled his experience with Lincoln when he escorted the congressman to Dedham for a speech.

He was as sober a man in point of expression as I ever saw. In the [train] he scarcely said a word to one of us. He seemed uneasy. . . . I should say the atmosphere of Boston was not congenial to him. We took him to one of the most elegant houses in the town of Dedham, and here he seemed still less . . . at home. The thing began to look rather blue for us. When we went over to the hall it was not much better. It was a small hall and only about half full; for Mr. Lincoln had not spoken in Boston yet, and there was nothing in his name particularly to attract. But at last he arose to speak, and almost instantly there was a change.

His indifferent manner vanished as soon as he opened his mouth. He went right to work. He wore a black alpaca sack [coat] and he turned up the sleeves of this, and then the cuffs of his shirt. Next he loosened his necktie, and soon after he took it off altogether. All the time he was gaining upon his audience. He soon had it as by a spell. I never saw men more delighted. His style was the most familiar and off-hand possible. His eye had lighted up and changed the whole expression of his countenance. He began to bubble out with humor. But the chief charm of his address lay in the homely way he made his points. There was no attempt at eloquence or finish of style. But, for plain pungency of humor, it would have been difficult to surpass his speech.[78]

The *Old Colony Republican* described Lincoln's performance in Taunton on September 21, 1848.

Argument and anecdote, wit and wisdom, hymns and prophecies came flying before the audience like wild game before the fierce hunter of the prairie. It was altogether an admirable speech . . . in a style that will long be remembered.[79]

In Worcester, Lincoln had dinner at the handsome home of Mayor Levi Lincoln. Neither man was a genealogist, so they never discovered that they were descendants of the same Samuel Lincoln who had come to Hingham, Massachusetts, in 1637. Here, too, his speech was a success. Henry J. Gardiner, a future governor of Massachusetts, never forgot it.

He repeated anecdotes, told stories admirable in humor and in point, interspersed with true eloquence which constantly brought down the house. His sarcasm of Cass, Van Buren and the Democratic Party was inimitable. Whenever he attempted to stop, the shouts of "Go on! Go on!" were deafening. He probably spoke for over an hour, but so great was the enthusiasm, time could not be measured.[80]

When he mentioned slavery in his speeches, Lincoln said that Massachusetts and Illinois were in agreement on preventing its expansion, but people in Illinois did not "keep so con-stantly thinking about it." In Boston, Lincoln spoke at the Tremont Temple on the same program with William Seward, former governor of New York. Seward's entire speech was devoted to slavery. Walking back to the Tremont House with Seward, Lincoln was silent, thoughtful. "I reckon you are right," he finally said. "We have got to deal with this slavery question, got to give much more attention to it hereafter than we have been doing."[81]

Perhaps the best tribute to Congressman Lincoln, the talented stump speaker from Illinois, was the notice that appeared in the pages of the Boston *Atlas* on September 16, 1848.

HON. ABRAHAM LINCOLN—In answer to many applications which we daily receive from many different parts of the State, for this gentleman to speak, we have to say that he left Boston on Saturday morning, on his way home to Illinois.[82]

*Ambrotype portrait of Lincoln
made by Abraham Byers
at Beardstown, Illinois,
May 7, 1858.
(Photo: Lloyd Ostendorf)*

CHAPTER FIVE

Lincoln went back to Illinois by steamer from Buffalo. Before he sailed, he visited Niagara Falls, which stirred philosophical thoughts.

. . . By what mysterious power is it that millions and millions are drawn from all parts of the world to gaze upon Niagara Falls? There is no mystery about the thing itself. . . . Its power to excite reflection, and emotion, is its great charm. . . . It calls up the indefinite past. When Columbus first sought this continent—when Christ suffered on the cross—when Moses led Israel through the Red-Sea—nay, even, when Adam first came from the hand of his Maker—then as now, Niagara was roaring here. The eyes of that species of extinct giants, whose bones fill the mounds of America, have gazed on Niagara, as ours do now. Co[n]temporary with the whole race of men, and older than the first man, Niagara is strong, and fresh to-day as ten thousand years ago. The Mammoth and Mastodon—now so long dead, have gazed on Niagara. In that long—long time, [Niagara was] never still for a single moment. Never dried, never froze, never slept, never rested.[83]

A few years later Lincoln visited Chicago and spent the night at the home of Norman Judd, chief attorney for the Chicago, Rock Island & Pacific Railroad. Watching twilight descend on Lake Michigan stirred Lincoln to similar philosophic thoughts. Years later, the evening remained one of Judd's most vivid memories.

Until quite late we sat on the broad piazza, looking out on the lovely scene. Vessels were availing themselves of a fine breeze to leave the harbor and the lake was studded with many a white sail. I remember that a flock of sea-gulls were flying along the beach, dipping their beaks and white-lined wings in the foam. While we sat there, the great white moon appeared on the rim of the eastern horizon and slowly crept above the water. Mr. Lincoln seemed carried away from all thought of the jars and turmoil of earth. In that mild pleasant voice, attuned to harmony with his surroundings, he began to speak of the mystery which for ages enshrouded and shut out those distant worlds above us from our own, of the poetry and beauty which was seen and felt by seers of old when they contemplated Orion and Arcturus as they wheeled around the earth in their nightly course.[84]

Less than a year after Lincoln returned from Congress, in February 1849, his second son, Eddie, died. Some biographers believe that this loss was the beginning of Lincoln's search for faith. He had heretofore shown little interest in organized religion. The following year, when his father was on his deathbed, he wrote a moving letter to his stepbrother John Johnston, with whom the old pioneer was living.

> I sincerely hope father may recover his health. But at all events tell him to remember to call upon and confide in our great and good and merciful Maker, who will not turn away from him in any extremity. He notes the fall of a sparrow and numbers the hairs of our heads and He will not forget the dying man who puts his trust in Him.[85]

Two more sons, Willie and Tad, arrived to help heal the wound of Eddie's death. With a growing family to support, Lincoln concentrated on his legal career and admitted that he had "almost lost interest in politics." But in 1854 a new upheaval over slavery shook the nation. "The Little Giant," Senator Stephen A. Douglas of Illinois, sponsored the Kansas-Nebraska Act, which repealed the Missouri Compromise of 1820 and permitted slavery to expand into the western territories on the basis of popular or "squatter" sovereignty. Lincoln attacked Douglas for what he considered a fundamental break with the philosophy of the Founding Fathers, who had tried to build barriers to the expansion of slavery into the fabric of the Republic, hoping the "peculiar institution" would die out naturally. Lincoln soon became the leading midwestern spokesman for the new Republican Party, a fusion of Whigs and antislavery Democrats. In 1856 he traveled to Kalamazoo, Michigan, to address a rally of 10,000 on behalf of John Frémont, the Republicans' first presidential candidate. Speaking from an old Indian mound in Bronson Park, he urged Democrats to help him rescue "the great principle of equality."[86]

Around this time, Lincoln wrote a letter to his friend Joshua F. Speed in which he recalled his trip from Louisville in 1841. But now his feelings about slavery had been transformed by time and events.

In 1841 you and I had together a tedious low-water trip on a steamboat from Louisville to St. Louis. You may remember, as I well do, that from Louisville to the mouth of the Ohio there were on board ten or a dozen slaves shackled together with irons. That sight was a continued torment to me, and I see something like it every time I touch the Ohio or any other slave border.[87]

The word "Republican" evoked fierce hostility in many places in Illinois, where the party was identified with the hated abolitionists. Lincoln encountered this animosity in 1856 where he least expected it—in Petersburg, the town where many of his old friends from New Salem days lived. Young Henry B. Rankin, Lincoln's clerk, witnessed the confrontation.

As Lincoln mounted the platform in the court house yard, the crowd began shouting insults. Lincoln stood before them, silent, motionless, watching them. Fully half an hour passed. I never spent one that seemed longer. I saw no movement by Lincoln during that time except a change in the position of his arms and the occasional closing and unclosing of his right hand.

Then came a let-up in the roar of voices. The crowd had almost shouted itself out. Lincoln began speaking in a very low voice. Even those nearest him could scarcely hear what he said. Those farther away could only see the movement of his lips. Curiosity began to get the better of them one and all and the few who wanted to hear what he had to say began to call for silence. Gradually the noisy mob relapsed into complete quiet and *listened*.[88]

On June 16, 1858, the Illinois Republican State Convention adopted without a dissenting vote a resolution declaring that "Abraham Lincoln is the first and only choice of the Republicans of Illinois for the United States Senate, as the successor of Stephen A. Douglas."[89]

Lincoln's law office.
With a growing family to support,
Lincoln concentrated on his
legal career and admitted
that he had "almost lost
interest in politics."
(Photo: Arthur Shay)

In 1858 the Illinois Republican
State Convention unanimously
named Lincoln their candidate
for the United States Senate.
Here in the Illinois House of Representatives
he read his acceptance speech
to friends, including the famous
"house divided" statement. (Photo: Arthur Shay)

Lincoln called together a caucus of his friends and read his acceptance speech to them. Everyone except his law partner, William Herndon, begged him to remove one paragraph, which they said was too radical. Herndon said: "Lincoln, deliver that speech as read and it will make you President." Lincoln told his friends: "If it is decreed that I should go down because of this speech, then let me go down linked to the truth." So he rose and spoke the fateful words.

A house divided against itself cannot stand. I believe this government cannot endure, permanently half slave and half free. I do not expect the Union to be dissolved—I do not expect the house to fall—but I do expect it will cease to be divided. It will become all one thing or all the other.[90]

Lincoln challenged Douglas to a series of seven debates. From Freeport in the north to Jonesboro in the south, from Charleston in the east to Quincy and Alton along Illinois's western border, to Galesburg and Ottawa in the center of the state the contestants journeyed, attracting immense, tremendously excited crowds. It was the greatest political and social spectacle of the era. Reporters hurried from all parts of the nation to cover it. One of the best descriptions of the crowds appeared in the New York *Evening Post.*

Over long, weary miles of hot and dusty prairie, from Charleston on the procession of eager partisans came—on foot, on horseback, in wagons drawn by horses or mules; men, women and children, old and young; the half sick, just out of the last "shake"[of fever]; children in arms, infants at the maternal fount, pushing on in clouds of dust and beneath a blazing sun; settling down at the town where the meeting is with hardly a chance for sitting, and even less opportunity for eating, waiting in anxious groups for hours at the places of speaking, talking, discussing, litigious, vociferous, while the roar of artillery, the music of bands, the waving of banners, the huzzas of the crowds, as delegation after delegation appears; the cry of peddlers, vending all sorts of wares, from an infallible cure of "agur" to a monstrous watermelon in slices to suit purchasers—combining to render the occasion one scene of confusion and commotion. The hour of one arrives, and a perfect rush is made for the grounds; a column of dust rising to the heavens and fairly deluging those who are hurrying on through it. Then the speakers come, with flags, and banners, and music, surrounded by cheering partisans. Their arrival at the grounds and immediate approach to the stand is [sic] the signal for shouts that rend the heavens. They are introduced to the audience amid prolonged and enthusiastic cheers; they are interrupted by frequent applause, and they sit down finally amid the same uproarious demonstrations. The audience sit or stand patiently throughout, and as the last word is spoken, make a break for their homes, first hunting up lost members of their families, gathering their scattered wagon loads together, and as the daylight fades away, entering again upon the broad prairies and slowly picking their way back "to the place of beginning!"[91]

At Quincy, on the Mississippi River, Carl Schurz, German university graduate and liberal Republican, saw Lincoln for the first time.

Mr. Lincoln was to open with an allowance of one hour. His voice was not musical, rather high-keyed, and apt to turn into a shrill treble in moments of excitement; but it was not positively disagreeable. It had an exceedingly penetrating, far-reaching quality. . . . His gesture was awkward. He swung his long arms sometimes in a very ungraceful manner. Now and then he would, to give particular emphasis to a point, bend his knees and body with a sudden downward jerk, and then shoot up again with a vehemence that raised him to his tiptoes and made him look much taller than he really was.

There was, however, in all he said, a tone of earnest truthfulness, of elevated, noble sentiment, and of kindly sympathy, which added greatly to the strength of his argument, and became, as in the course of his speech he touched upon the moral side of the question in debate, powerfully impressive. Even when attacking his opponent with keen satire or invective, which, coming from any other speaker, would have sounded bitter and cruel, there was still a certain something in his utterance making his hearers feel that those thrusts

65

came from a reluctant heart, and that he would much rather have treated his foe as a friend.[92]

Ward Hill Lamon recalled an incident that revealed Lincoln's total absorption in the battle.

In the Charleston debate, Douglas charged that Lincoln had failed to support the war with Mexico when he was in Congress. Lincoln angrily replied that it was a "perversion of the facts." He had opposed a declaration of war but once it was declared, he had voted for "any proposition looking to the comfort of our poor fellows who were maintaining the dignity of our flag." I was at the time sitting on the stand beside Hon. O. B. Ficklin, who had served in Congress with Mr. Lincoln in 1847. Mr. Lincoln reached back and took Ficklin by the coat collar and in no gentle manner, lifted him from his seat as if he had been a kitten, and said: "Fellow-citizens, here is Ficklin, who was at that time in Congress with me and he knows it is a lie." He shook Ficklin until his teeth chattered. Fearing that he would shake Ficklin's head off, I grasped Mr. Lincoln's hand and broke his grip. Mr. Ficklin reeled back to his seat and Lincoln continued his address.[93]

Mary Lincoln's cousin, William M. Dickson, asked the contestants to estimate each other.

Mr. Lincoln had a high admiration for the abilities of Mr. Douglas, but he thought him in debate and in politics adroit, unscrupulous, and of an amazing audacity. "It is impossible," said he, "to get the advantage of him; even if he is worsted, he so bears himself that the people are bewildered and uncertain as to who has the better of it."

Some weeks after this conversation with Mr. Lincoln, I met Mr. Douglas, and drew from him his opinion of Mr. Lincoln. His very words, terse, and emphatic as they were, I give: "Of all the ———— Whig rascals about Springfield, Abe Lincoln is the ablest and most honest."[94]

Mary Lincoln also had an emphatic opinion of the debaters.

Mr. Douglas is a very little, *little* giant by the side of my tall Kentuckian and intellectually my husband towers above Douglas just as he does physically.[95]

Chatting with his law partner, Lincoln himself gave one of the best analyses of the difference between him and Stephen Douglas.

"Give me your little pen-knife, with its short blade, and hand me that old jack-knife, lying on the table," Lincoln said. Opening the blade of the pen-knife, he said: "You see, this blade at the point travels rapidly, but only through a short space; while the long blade of the jack-knife moves no faster but through a much greater space. Just so with my mind. I may not emit ideas as rapidly as others, but when I do throw off a thought it has force enough to cut its own way and travel a greater distance."[96]

The intense feeling aroused by the debates is visible in this incident, which occurred in Springfield.

The speaker's stand was erected against the state house fence. Lincoln stood six or eight feet south of the corner. There were five or six hundred men on the east side and the crowd overflowed around the corner, to the north side. A well-dressed, self-important looking man on a fine horse pushed his way in, up close to Lincoln and when Lincoln said he was not in favor with interfering with slavery where it then existed, this man said in a loud voice so all could hear, "How would you like to sleep with a nigger?" Lincoln stopped and without replying looked the man in the eyes with a sad, pitiful look as if he felt sorry for him. The man hung his head, turning to get away, but the crowd held him, spitting all over him. Lincoln continued his talk as if he had not been interrupted.[97]

Lincoln was an important man now, far different from the raw, uneducated boy who had drifted into New Salem. But there were moments when his mind leaped back over the years to the Old Concord Burial Ground near Petersburg, where Ann Rutledge lay. During the campaign against Douglas in 1858, he wrote a poem for the daughter of an innkeeper in Winchester, Illinois.

To Rosa—

> You are young, and I am older;
> > You are hopeful, I am not—
> Enjoy life, ere it grows colder—
> > Pluck the roses ere they rot.
> Teach your beau to heed the lay—
> > That sunshine soon is lost in shade—
> That *now*'s as good as any day—
> > To take thee, Rosa, ere she fade.

Not everyone was impressed by Lincoln. A New Jersey Democratic paper called him "the brainless Bob-o-Link of the Prairies."[99] Lincoln himself liked to recall an incident in Decatur. An Old Democrat from "Egypt" approached Mr. Lincoln and said: "So you're Abe Lincoln?"

"Yes, that is my name."

"They say you're a self-made man."

"Well, yes; what there is of me is self-made."

"Well, all I've got to say," observed the man, after a careful survey of the Republican candidate, "is that it was a damned bad job!"[100]

Although he lost the fight for Douglas' Senate seat, Lincoln continued to be in demand as a speaker. In 1859 he visited Council Bluffs, Iowa, ostensibly to investigate some property he had acquired there in payment for a legal fee. He was scarcely in the city when Republicans organized a rally and asked him to address them. Before the speech Lincoln went up to the highest point on the Oakland Avenue bluffs, since known as Mount Lincoln, where he had a panoramic view of the Missouri river valley. Later that day he met Grenville Dodge, an engineer who had been surveying the best route for a railroad to the Pacific. Lincoln told Dodge that in his opinion the railroad was the most important challenge confronting the nation.

> He ingeniously extracted a great deal of information from me about the country beyond the [Missouri] River, the climate, the character of the soil, the resources. When the long conversation ended, I realized that most of the things I had been holding as secrets for my employer [the Rock Island, Chicago & Pacific Railroad] had been given to him.[101]

Lincoln's genius for places shone out in his talk with Grenville Dodge, commented Carl Sandburg. Four years later, as President, Lincoln chose Council Bluffs as the terminus for the Union Pacific transcontinental railroad.

A trip to Kansas in 1859 involved as rugged traveling as Lincoln ever encountered. Here is how newspaperman Albert D. Richardson reacted to him.

In the imaginative language of the frontier, Troy was a town—possibly a city—but, save a shabby frame courthouse, a tavern and a few shanties, its urban glories were visible only to the eye of faith. It was intensely cold. The sweeping prairie wind rocked the crazy buildings, and cut the faces of travelers like a knife. Mr. Lincoln's party arrived wrapped in buffalo robes.

Not more than forty people assembled in that little bare-walled courthouse. There was none of the magnetism of a multitude to inspire the long, angular, ungainly orator, who rose up behind a rough table. With little gesticulation—and that little ungraceful—he began, not to declaim, but to talk. In a conversational tone, he argued the question of slavery in the territories, in the language of an aver-age Ohio or New York farmer. I thought: "If the Illinoisans consider this a great man their ideas must be very peculiar." But, in ten or fifteen minutes, I was unconsciously and irresistibly drawn by the clearness and closeness of his argument. Link after link it was forged and welded, like a blacksmith's chain.

His anecdotes were felicitous and illustrative. Whenever he heard a man avow his determination to adhere unswervingly to the principles of the Democratic Party, it reminded him, he said, of a "little incident in Illinois." A lad, ploughing upon the prairie, asked his father in what direction he should strike a new furrow. The parent replied: "Steer for that yoke of oxen standing at the further end of the field." The father went away and the lad obeyed. But just as he started the oxen started also. He kept steering for them, and they continued to walk. He followed them entirely around the field, and came back to the starting-point, having furrowed a circle instead of a line.[102]

In Leavenworth, Kansas, Lincoln made two speeches. He stopped at the home of an old friend, Mark W. Delahay. In Mary Delahay's autograph album Lincoln left a record of his visit.

Dear Mary

With pleasure I write my name in your album. Ere long some younger man will be more happy to confer *his* name upon *you*.

Don't allow it, Mary, until fully assured that he is worthy of the happiness.[103]

In the fall of 1859 the Republicans of Wisconsin asked Lincoln to address the Wisconsin Agricultural Society in Milwaukee. To this appearance he added a visit to Beloit, where he spoke to the Republican Club. On the evening of the same day he addressed another meeting in nearby Janesville and stayed for the night at the home of William M. Tallman. Young Lucien Hanks, nephew of Mrs. Tallman, gave up his bed to Lincoln. Used to doubling up on the circuit, Lincoln said he had no objections to sharing the bed with Lucien. For young Lucien, this meant a sleepless night. "His body jerked and twitched spasmodically," he recalled. "His long legs would be kicking around, the subconscious effect probably of his vigorous speech but an hour or two before." Lucien retreated to a sofa in the hall.[104]

Lincoln told his Milwaukee audience:

It is said an Eastern monarch once charged his wise men to invent him a sentence to be ever in view, and which should be true and appropriate in all times and situations. They presented him the words: "And this, too, shall pass away." How much it expresses! How chastening in the hour of pride!— How consoling in the depths of affliction! "And this, too, shall pass away." And yet let us hope it is not *quite* true. Let us hope, rather, that by the best cultivation of the physical world, beneath and around us; and the intellectual and moral world within us, we shall secure an individual, social and political prosperity and happiness, whose course shall be onward and upward, and which, while the earth endures, shall not pass away.[105]

At the Agricultural Society fair he took hold of the handles of a plow and tipped it about as though the muscles of his shoulders knew all its proper motions and tingled to exercise them.[106]

In 1860 New York leaders invited Lincoln to speak in the Great Hall of the Cooper Union on
Astor Place in Manhattan. It had 2,000 revolving red leather chairs and twenty-eight gaslit chandeliers,
and was considered the most elegant auditorium in the world. (Photo: Sonntag/Coppolino)

CHAPTER SIX

Now the patricians of New York—the great financiers and merchants, the editors of the nation's most influential newspapers—decided that they wanted to hear and see this prairie politician named Lincoln. They invited him to speak in the Great Hall of the Cooper Union on Astor Place in Manhattan. Cooper Union, usually called Cooper Institute, was the first free night college for workingmen and women. The Great Hall had 2,000 revolving red leather chairs and twenty-eight gaslit chandeliers. It was considered the most elegant auditorium in the world.

Lincoln spent long hours preparing his speech. His chief opponent for the Republican nomination for the presidency was suave William Seward, now one of New York's U.S. senators. Lincoln was determined to impress these easterners, who were so quick to dismiss westerners as ignorant backwoodsmen. But he concentrated on his speech, which was the most carefully researched, closely reasoned argu-

ment he had yet constructed against the expansion of slavery. He paid little or no attention to his appearance. Lincoln had long since concluded there was little clothes could do to improve his gaunt, lanky physique.

As he stepped to the podium on the snowy night of February 27, 1860, the audience's reaction was almost universally negative. "The first impression . . . did nothing to contradict the expectation of something weird, rough and uncultivated," recalled George Haven Putnam. "The long ungainly figure, the large feet, the clumsy hands of which at the outset the author seemed to be unduly conscious; the long gaunt head capped by a shock of hair that seemed not to have been thoroughly brushed out. . . ."[107]

Others commented on his clothes. One said they were "the most unbecoming that a fiend's ingenuity could have devised for a tall gaunt man—a black frock coat, ill-setting and too short for him in the body, skirt and arms, a rolling collar, low down disclosing his long thin shriveled throat."

Lincoln's accent did not help matters. According to the *New York Times*, he began with the words: "Mr. Cheerman." A titter ran through the audience.[108]

A literary critic of the day recalled thinking:

Ole fellow, you won't do; it's all very well for the Wild West but this will never go down in New York. But pretty soon he began to get into his subject; he straightened up, made regular and graceful gestures; his face lighted as with an inward fire; the whole man was transfigured. I forgot his clothes, his personal appearance and his individual peculiarities. Presently I was on my feet with the rest, yelling like a wild Indian, cheering this wonderful man.[109]

No fewer than four New York papers reprinted the Cooper Union speech with its magnificent closing words: "Let us have faith that right makes might and in that faith dare to do our duty as we understand it."[110]

Earlier in the day Lincoln had been given a tour of New York by his hosts. They took him into the slums of the Five Points, one of the poorest and most lawless sections of the city. The party stopped at the Five Points Mission, where orphaned slum children were fed and given a rudimentary education. A Sunday school class was in session, and the superintendent asked Lincoln to speak to the children.

Lincoln described what happened next.

I told them I did not know anything about talking to Sunday Schools but Mr. Pease said many of the children were friendless and homeless, and that a few words would do them good. And so I rose to speak. . . . I thought of the time when I had been pinched by terrible poverty. And so I told them that I had been poor; that I remembered when my toes stuck out through my broken shoes in winter; when my arms were out at the elbows; when I shivered with the cold. And I told them there was only one rule; that was, always to do the very best you can. I told them that I had always tried to do the very best I could; and that if they would follow that rule, they would get along somehow. . . .

Lincoln was unable to continue. He left the mission, his eyes filled with tears. "I'm glad we came," he said. "I shall never forget this as long as I live."[111]

Erastus Corning, president of the New York Central Railroad, had heard Lincoln's speech at Cooper Union in New York and was deeply impressed. The next morning he hurried down to the Astor House and was introduced to the speaker.

"Mr. Lincoln," Corning said, "I understand that in Illinois you win all your lawsuits."

Lincoln laughed softly. "Oh, no, Mr. Corning, that is not true," he replied.

"Would you accept an offer from the New York Central," continued Mr. Corning, "to become its general counsel at a salary of $10,-000 a year?"

This proposition was as amazing as it was sudden. Members of the Lincoln party were struck dumb with surprise. Lincoln lapsed into a deep study.

"Why, Mr. Corning," he said at last, "what would I do with $10,000 a year? It would ruin my family to have that much income. I don't believe that I had better consider it."[112]

The success of the Cooper Union speech prompted Republicans to invite Lincoln on a speaking tour of New England. Here is his itinerary.

Tuesday, February 28th, speech at Providence, R.I., evening.

Wednesday, February 29th, no speech, en route to New Hampshire.

Thursday, March 1st, speech at Concord, N.H., afternoon; speech at Manchester, N.H., evening.

Friday, March 2nd, speech at Dover, N.H., evening.

Saturday, March 3rd, speech at Exeter, N.H., evening.

Sunday, March 4th, spent day with son Robert at Exeter, N.H.

Monday, March 5th, speech at Hartford, Conn., evening.

Tuesday, March 6th, speech at New Haven, Conn., evening.

Wednesday, March 7th, speech at Meriden, Conn., evening.

Thursday, March 8th, speech at Woonsocket, R.I., evening.

Friday, March 9th, speech at Norwich, Conn., evening.

Saturday, March 10th, speech at Bridgeport, Conn., evening.[113]

In Dover, New Hampshire, after his speech, Lincoln walked a block up Church Street, crossed Locust, and went to bed in the large northeast corner chamber of George Mathewson's beautiful home. He arose from his brief sleep at about five o'clock Saturday morning, made his own bed, and went for a walk before the household awoke. That "redding up" of his room was regarded not as a mark of Western greenness, but as a token of Lincoln's thoughtfulness.

Lincoln had his morning shave at the hands of Thomas Law in the second-floor barber shop on the north corner of Dover's Central and Orchard Streets. Law often told about his critical job scraping over the mountains and valleys of the rugged face.[114]

As important to Lincoln as the political opportunity of his New England tour was the chance to visit his son Robert, who was spending a year at Exeter Academy, preparing for the entrance examinations to Harvard. Inevitably Lincoln was invited to speak soon after he arrived. One of Robert Lincoln's fellow pupils later recalled how the man from Illinois impressed the audience.

Mr. Lincoln sat down in a chair reserved for him, and, with some difficulty, succeeded in arranging his long legs. I saw a man whose face impressed me as one of the most interesting as well as one of the saddest and most melancholy faces that I had ever seen. His hair was rumpled, his neckwear was all awry, he sat somewhat bent in the chair, and altogether presented a very remarkable, and, to us, disappointing appearance.

Judge John C. Underwood was introduced as the first speaker, and delivered, as I am told, a very able speech. I confess I heard none of it, nor did those of my friends who sat near me. We sat and stared at Mr. Lincoln. We whispered to each other: "Isn't it too bad Bob's father is so homely? Don't you feel sorry for him?"

At last, Judge Underwood concluded his speech, and Mr. Lincoln was presented to us. He rose slowly, untangled those long legs from their contact with the rounds of the chair, drew himself up to his full height of six feet, four inches, and began his speech. Not ten minutes had passed before his uncouth appearance was absolutely forgotten by us boys and, I believe, by all of that large audience. For an hour and a half he held the closest attention of every person present. There was no more pity for our friend Bob.[115]

There was a little gathering of Academy boys in Bob's room on Sunday evening. Bob remarked that one of the party, Henry Cluskey, played the banjo. "Does he?" said Lincoln in his high-pitched voice. "Where is the banjo?" "In my room," replied Cluskey. "Can't you get it?" "Oh, I don't think you would care for it, Mr. Lincoln." "Oh, yes. Go get it!" And so the owner of the banjo went and fetched it from his room several blocks away, and played upon it. Lincoln listened with unaffected pleasure. "Robert," he said, "you ought to have one." What the youngsters chiefly remembered about their friend's father was that when he talked with Bob, or the boys gathered around, the deep seams of his face broke into a series of twinkling lines. Every boy was at once drawn to him.[116]

In Manchester, New Hampshire, Lincoln spoke at Smith's Opera House to an overflow crowd. The following morning he accepted an invitation to visit the Amoskeag Mills, one of the largest and best known in the country. A young machinist, Edwin P. Richardson, was sent for to escort Lincoln through the various departments.

Thinking I was simply wanted to make some repairs about the machinery, I did not take the trouble to change my clothes or even to wash my begrimed face and hands. Judge, then, of my surprise upon entering the private office, of seeing an extremely tall and rugged man standing before me, the very speaker I had listened to the evening before with so much interest. Mr. Straw introduced him to me, but when Mr. Lincoln held out one of his great hands to clasp mine, I shrank back, saying in a tone that I know could not have been entirely free from tremor:

"My hands are hardly fit to take yours, Mr. Lincoln, so—"

"Young man, the hand of honest toil is never too grimy for Abe Lincoln to clasp."

You may rest assured it was a good, long, hearty grip that he gave me, until I felt my hand ache under the pressure of his mighty grasp.

"Ed," said Mr. Straw, "you will show

Mills at Manchester, N.H.,
where Lincoln told a machinist,
"Young man, the hand of honest toil
is never too grimy for
Abe Lincoln to clasp."
(Photo: Paul Avis)

Mr. Lincoln over the mills, and explain anything he may wish to know about them."

Again I hesitated, stammering: "I shall be only too glad to do so, if Mr. Lincoln will but wait until I can wash up and change my clothes." Fixing those large, mournful eyes upon me, the future President said in a tone that was not to be misunderstood:

"Young man, go just as you are."[117]

Judge David Cross recalled one incident in Lincoln's speech in Manchester.

Rev. Mr. Foss, a violent Abolitionist and an able and honest man, occasionally interrupted him and asked him questions. After a while the audience cried, "Throw him out." Mr. Lincoln replied, "No, no, let him stay, he is just the man I want to see and to answer. Now, my friend, what is your question? Let's talk together, I *want* you to jaw back." Mr. Foss asked Mr. Lincoln several questions and Lincoln replied, and soon Mr. Foss was applauding with the rest of the audience, and after the meeting was over, Foss took Lincoln by the hand and thanked him and said, "You are the only man that has ever talked to me in this way and I am not sure but you are right."[118]

Equality of opportunity as he had experienced it in his own life was a theme Lincoln emphasized in New Haven.

I am not ashamed to confess that twenty-five years ago I was a hired laborer, mauling rails at work on a flatboat—just what might happen to any poor man's son! I want every man to have a chance.[119]

CHAPTER SEVEN

Back in Illinois, the Republican State Convention met in Springfield and nominated Lincoln as its candidate for the presidency. Then came an incident that carried him back to his New Salem days.

The rail committee, headed by John Hanks, pressed through the crowd with

Abraham Lincoln in front of his Springfield residence after a Republican rally, August 8, 1860. (Photo: Chicago Historical Society)

several rails, carried them to the platform, and standing them up stood by them. Without further word the crowd, into which Lincoln had pressed his way some distance, commenced to shout "Identify your work." He was at once seized upon and carried in the arms and over the heads of the crowd to the platform and placed beside the rails. Then the Convention, being again seated, shouted, "Identify your work! Identify your work!" Turning to Mr. Hanks and the committee, and looking at the rails, Mr. Lincoln asked: "Where did you get the rails?" Mr. Hanks replied: "At the farm you improved down on the Sangamon." "Well," said Lincoln, "that was a long time ago. However, it is possible I may have split these rails, but I cannot identify them." Again the Convention shouted, "Identify your work! Identify your work!" At this time the care visible on Mr. Lincoln's face gave way to a pleasant smile and he asked, "What kind of timber are they?" The committee replied, "Honey locust and black walnut." "Well," said Lincoln, his smile increasing, "that is lasting timber, and it may be that I split the rails." Then

he seemed to examine the rails critically, his smile all the time increasing, until his contagious merriment was visible, and he said, "Well, boys, I can only say I have split a great many better looking ones."

This tactful turn was met by a storm of approval, and three times three were then given, and three more for "Honest Abraham Lincoln, the rail candidate, our next President."[120]

Law clerk Henry B. Rankin gives us this picture of Lincoln as he learned he had won the Republican nomination at the party's convention in Chicago.

A few minutes later the second ballot came in, showing a gain of seventy-nine votes for Lincoln while Seward had only gained eleven votes. Just then Lincoln and several others came into the editorial rooms of the *Sangamo Journal.* The dispatch was handed to him. No one spoke a word. I can never forget the look that came on his face as he read it. At that moment he believed he would be nominated. It was only a short time by the watch— but it seemed long to the expectant friends in the *Journal* office—before the third ballot was handed in, and it was shouted: "Lincoln's nominated."

A merchant from Boston, Mass., who happened to be present and standing by Lincoln, suggested that Lincoln's life be written at once. Lincoln turned to the man [and] gravely said: "My friend, I do not see much in my life as yet to write about."[121]

Lincoln's election as President inspired furious antagonism in the South. Some southerners talked of capturing Washington and preventing his inauguration. This threat angered Illinoisans, Democrats as well as Republicans. While visiting Charleston, Illinois after his election, D. W. Chambers gave Lincoln a message from a mutual friend, a lifelong Democrat named Pete Miller.

Miller had not voted for Lincoln, but he wanted him to know that if anyone attempted to prevent his inauguration on March 4, he would "shed the last drop of his blood" in support of Lincoln's claim. Lincoln apparently had reason to doubt Pete's extreme commitment. He told Chambers their old friend was more likely to react like a certain young man who

was going to war. "His two loving and admiring sisters had made an embroidered belt for him to wear, and when they had it completed, they asked him what motto they should put upon it. 'Victory or death?' 'No, no,' says he, 'don't put it quite that strong. Put it 'Victory or get hurt pretty bad.' "[122]

Lincoln spent most of his time between his election and inauguration conferring with politicians about his Cabinet and other appointments and working on his inaugural address. Meanwhile, the South was moving toward secession. On one of his last days in Illinois, he went down to Coles County to say good-bye to his stepmother, Sarah Bush Lincoln. Everyone in the little village of Farmington flocked to see him. Neighbors, with frontier helpfulness, rushed to prepare a dinner. Baked turkeys and chickens, cakes and pies appeared as if by magic. Tables made of planks on sawhorses were "set clear from one end of the house to another." Everyone sat down to dinner with the President-elect. Outside, little girls put their feet in his overshoes, which he had left beside the door. "Mr. Lincoln was simplicity itself. He seemed to enjoy it so much that his face was continually lit up with a sunny smile," recalled R. H. Osborne, the village schoolteacher. Finally it was time to go.

I was in the room when Mr. Lincoln was getting ready to take his farewell of his stepmother, about three o'clock in the afternoon. On the bed was a fur cape which he had brought her as a present. Sarah Bush Lincoln was seated in a rocking chair near him and while he was talking to those who were in the room one of his hands clasped the rocking chair. He put his arm gently about her and it was at this time she said: "Abe, I'll never see you alive again. They will kill you."[123]

On his way back to Springfield, Lincoln stopped in Charleston and greeted old friends in the Town Hall. He seemed keenly aware that he was departing from the land and people that had nurtured him. He obviously felt a need for one last encounter with them.

In the audience were many persons who had known him as the stalwart young ex-driver when his father's family drove into Illinois from southern Indiana. One man had brought with him a horse which the President elect had recovered for him

in a suit; another was able to recite from personal recollection the thrilling details of the famous wrestling match between Lincoln the flatboatman and Daniel Needham. All had some reminiscence of his early manhood to relate.[124]

The crowd in some way expected to hear him speak. He took a position on the stand and gravely said: "You my friends, are anxious to hear from me, what I think of the outlook for the future, but I am equally anxious with you to see what lies before us. You will have to excuse me from saying more, but if it will be any gratification to you, I shall be glad to take each one of you by the hand." The crowd then moved past him and he gave to each a cordial warm-hearted grasp.[125]

Lincoln's complete absence of ostentation and his frontier self-reliance was illustrated on the morning of his departure from Springfield.

Having leased his home, Lincoln was staying at the Chenery House, the leading hostelry in Springfield. In the hotel office he roped his trunks with his own hands and took some of the hotel cards, on the

The day before his 52nd birthday
Lincoln departed Springfield
from this railroad station.
"I now leave," he said, "not knowing
when, or whether ever, I may return,
with a task before me greater than
that which rested on the
shoulders of Washington."
(Photo: Arthur Shay)

back of which he wrote:

A. Lincoln

White House

Washington, D.C.

and tacked them on the trunks. In due time the omnibus backed up in front of the hotel and he left for the depot.[126]

The morning of February 11, 1861, the day before Lincoln's 52nd birthday, dawned over Springfield through leaden skies in a cold, gray, misty air. Many citizens and visitors gathered at the Wabash Station to witness Lincoln's departure. He and his friends arrived in good time and entered the car reserved for them, not stopping in the waiting-room. Those were tense moments for the people who waited without. Schedule time for starting was near. Impatient reporters were anxious lest they might miss a chance to wire the last words of the President-elect from Springfield.

At the last moment Lincoln appeared at the rear door of the car. He paused as if surprised at the sudden burst of applause occasioned by his appearance, and removing his hat, stepped out on the platform, bowing right and left, and remaining silent until the salute ceased. His manner was calm and self-contained, yet his voice was tremulous with suppressed emotions, while strong emphasis marked many words and sentences.

"My friends—No one not in my situation can appreciate my feelings of sadness at this parting. To this place, and the kindness of this people I owe everything. Here I have lived a quarter of a century, and have passed from a young to an old man. Here my children were born and one lies buried.

"I now leave, not knowing when, or whether ever, I may return, with a task before me greater than that which rested on the shoulders of Washington.

"Without the aid of that Divine Being who ever aided him, who controls mine and all destinies, I cannot succeed. With that assistance I cannot fail.

"Trusting in Him who can go with me and remain with you, and be everywhere for good, let us confidently hope that all will be well.

"To His care commending you, as I hope in your prayers you will commend me, I bid you, friends and neighbors, an affectionate farewell."

The last sentence was spoken in lower tones, with a yearning tenderness in his voice most unusual to him; and, with its closing words, he bowed low and with firmly compressed lips whose silence meant so much to those who knew him best, turned from his position on the platform and stood at the open door, while the train, just starting, moved slowly, bearing him away from us forever, through that cold, gray misty haze of rain.[127]

CHAPTER EIGHT

By this time secession fever was sweeping the South and the border states. The situation was grave, and Lincoln's twelve-day railroad journey to Washington followed a zigzag route across Indiana, Ohio, into western Pennsylvania, back into Ohio and then into New York, New Jersey, and eastern Pennsylvania. The purpose was to rally as much of the country as possible, without giving the South a chance to accuse the President-elect of starting the war. The train made numerous stops, more than forty in the three days it took to reach Pittsburgh, where Lincoln made a speech on the tariff. At most of the stops Lincoln did little more than thank the people for displaying their loyalty to the Union and promise them, with their support, he would do his best to get them and the country "through the storm."

During the presidential campaign a young girl, Grace Bedell of Westfield, New York, had written to Lincoln, urging him to grow a beard. On February 16 Lincoln's train stopped at Westfield, and a Philadelphia *Inquirer* reporter recorded the scene.

> . . . Mr. Lincoln greeted a large crowd of ladies, and several thousand of the sterner sex. Addressing the ladies, he said: I am glad to see you; I suppose you are to see me; but I certainly think I have the best of the bargain. (Applause.) Some three months ago, I received a letter from a young lady here; it was a very pretty letter, and she advised me to let my whiskers grow, so it would improve my personal appearance; acting partly upon her sugges-

tion, I have done so; and now, if she is here, I would like to see her; I think her name was Miss Barlly. A small boy, mounted on a post, with his mouth and eyes both wide open, cried out, "there she is, Mr. Lincoln," pointing to a beautiful girl with black eyes, who was blushing all over her fair face. The President left the car, and the crowd making way for him, he reached her, and gave her several hearty kisses, and amid the yells of delight from the excited crowd, he bade her good-bye, and on we rushed.[128]

Here is how another young girl, Lavinia Goodell, described Lincoln's tumultuous reception in New York City.

. . . O, 'Ria, 'Ria! What do you think; *I have seen "Abe"*—"Old Abe"—"Honest Old Abe" &c.—&c!!! The Trubyns and myself went over to some friends of theirs in New York where the procession passed.

We stood out on a balcony in front, where we had an excellent view of him. All the city was alive as at the era of the Prince of Wales. The President was obliged to ride with his hat off, so contin-

ual was the cheering and waving of kerchiefs. We were opposite the Fifth Ave. Hotel, which presented a brilliant appearance. "Abe" is much better looking than is represented. Is tall, has a long nose, is thin, energetic looking, smiling and pleasant, frank and open. He looks young, his hair being perfectly black. Altogether I was quite favorably struck with him, and feel deeply interested in his welfare.[129]

As the presidential party drew closer to Washington, and the news reached it that Jefferson Davis had taken the oath of office as president of the Confederate States of America, Lincoln's speeches grew more serious. At Independence Hall in Philadelphia he talked about the meaning of America.

I am filled with deep emotion at finding myself standing here in the place where were collected together the wisdom, the patriotism, the devotion to principle, from which sprang the institutions under which we live. You have kindly suggested to me that in my hands is the task of restoring peace to our distracted country. All the political sentiments I entertain have been drawn, so far as I have been able to draw them, from the sentiments which originated, and were given to the world from this hall in which we stand. I have never had a feeling politically that did not spring from the sentiments embodied in the Declaration of Independence. [Great cheering.] I have often pondered over the dangers which were incurred by the men who assembled here and adopted that Declaration of Independence—I have pondered over the toils that were endured by the officers and soldiers of the army, who achieved that independence. [Applause.] I have often inquired of myself, what great principle or idea it was that kept this confederacy so long together. It was not the mere matter of the separation of the colonies from the mother land; but something in that Declaration giving liberty, not alone to the people of this country, but hope to the world for all future time. [Great applause.][130]

Having escaped a Baltimore assassination plot by traveling incognito on a special train, Lincoln slipped into tense, uneasy Washington, D.C., on February 23, 1861. In his inaugural address, he urged the seceded southern states to return to the union. "In your hands, my dissatisfied fellow countrymen, and not in mine, is the momentous issue of civil war." On April 12, 1861 at 4:30 a.m. the South replied by bombarding Fort Sumter at the mouth of Charleston harbor. The war had begun. For the next four years, Lincoln would be a virtual prisoner in the White House, seldom leaving it to journey beyond the immediate environs of the capital. But he brought with him the strength and the humor, the shrewdness and the sentiment of the people and the land he knew so well. "Surrounded by wealth, power, fashion, influence, by adroit politicians and artful schemers of every sort," his law partner William Herndon wrote, "Lincoln [did] not change a particle."[131]

President Lincoln's conversation was interlarded with rural images. "I will pitch into that like a dog at a root," he exclaimed when presented with a problem. "Well, I have got that job husked out," he sighed with relief on completing a perplexing presidential task. The sight of the diminutive Alexander H. Stephens, the Confederate Vice President, divesting himself of voluminous wraps moved him to comment:"That is the largest shucking for so small a nubbin that I ever saw." He referred to the Post Office Department's "cutting its own fodder." In reviewing some court martial proceedings he came upon the case of a condemned deserter who had escaped to Mexico; and apparently relieved that the man had gotten away, he observed: "We will condemn him as they used to sell hogs in Indiana—as they run."[132]

The correspondent of the *London Times* was introduced to him in the White House and wrote, "Mr. Lincoln put out his hand in a very friendly manner, and said, 'Mr. Russell, I am very glad to make your acquaintance, and to see you in this country. The *London Times* is one of the greatest powers in the world,—in fact, I don't know anything which has much more power,—unless perhaps it's the Mississippi.' "

He had seen that river as a flatboatman, as a Black Hawk war soldier, as a lawyer trying cases in cities overlooking it. His sentiment against disunion ran deeper be-cause disunion would have meant a split control, a divided allegiance to his great river.[133]

"Major, do you remember ever meeting me before?" President Lincoln asked Major Robert Anderson, the hero of Fort Sumter, when he came to the White House.

"No, Mr. President," Anderson replied.

"My memory is better than yours," Lincoln said. "You mustered me into the service of the United States in 1832 in the Black Hawk War."[134]

Talking to a friend who was concerned about Secretary of the Treasury Salmon P. Chase's ambition for the presidency, and who thought Lincoln should ask Chase to resign, Lincoln observed that Chase's department was functioning very well, and as long as it continued to do so he would not worry about Chase's presidential aspirations. The situation reminded him of a time when he and his step-brother were plowing a corn field in Indiana, he driving the horse and his step-brother guiding the plow. The horse, naturally lazy and slow, suddenly rushed across the field so fast the boys could hardly keep pace with him. On reaching the end of the furrow, Lincoln discovered an enormous chin fly fastened to the horse and knocked it off. His step-brother asked why he did that; Lincoln explained that he didn't want the horse bitten. "But, Abe," protested his step-brother, "that's all that made him go!"

"Now," said Lincoln, "if Mr. Chase has a presidential chin fly biting him, I'm not going to knock it off if it will make his department go."[135]

The necessity to wear gloves Mr. Lincoln regarded as an affliction, a violation of the statute against "cruelty to animals." At about the time of his third White House reception he had on a tight fitting pair of white kids. He saw approaching an old Illinois friend named Simpson, whom he welcomed with a genuine Sangamon County shake, which resulted in bursting his right glove with an audible sound.

Raising his brawny hand and looking at it with an indescribable expression, he said: "Well my old friend, this is a general bustification. You and I were never intended to wear these things."[136]

Lincoln's experience as a wrestler proved invaluable in his struggles with the Army of the Potomac's arrogant commander, General George B. McClellan. White House clerk William O. Stoddard recalled one encounter.

"Leave that and come with me. I am going over to McClellan's house." I arose at once, but did so without any reply whatever, for there was something in Mr. Lincoln's voice and manner that seemed to forbid any remarks on my part. Down we went and out, and the distance to be traveled was not long. He did not utter one word nor did I, for I was strongly impressed with the fact that there was something on his mind.

The house was reached and we were shown into a well-furnished front parlor with the usual fireplace and mantel and a centre table. I went over to the right and sat down in a chair, but the President took a seat in the middle of the room. He was calm, steady, even smiling, but in half a minute there was no room there at all. Only Abraham Lincoln, filling the place brimful. Our names had been carried upstairs, I knew, but long minutes went by and I felt the hot blood surging into my cheeks, hotter and hotter with every moment of what seemed to me a disrespectful waiting-time. Not so the great man over there beyond the table, for he was as cool and solid as ice. Then—for the hall door was open—a kind of jingle, and slow, descending footsteps were heard from the stairs. It was the great general himself, in full uniform, followed by his chief of staff, General Marcy, and an army colonel. In dress uniform with their swords they were a brilliant trio. General McClellan may have thought that he had come downstairs to receive the President formally and impressively, but he was altogether mistaken. He entered that parlor to be received there, very kindly, by President Abraham Lincoln, who somehow had taken possession and was the only man in the room.

The conference began almost immediately, for a kind of report of the situation and of plans was plainly called for. It was given, in a masterly way, by McClellan. He was a man of nerve strength, and I admired him as he went on into what was made more and more evidently a grand wrestling-match, with the control of the armies for the prize; also the future control of the political situation and the next Presidency of the United States. Lincoln listened well and he said little, at first. Then, a word at a time, he began to open, expanding visibly as he went on, and the match became intensely interesting. Grapple after grapple, tug, strain—down you go! Perfect accord, perfect good-will, perfect good manners, not a trace of excitement on either side. There was, in fact, a mutual yielding of many points under discussion, but at the end of it they had all been surrendered by General McClellan, with the courteous assistance of his handsome and capable chief of staff, General Marcy. A close came, and Mr. Lincoln and I were ceremoniously shown to the door. The parlor we left behind us was still, to my mind, full of Mr. Lincoln, although he had walked out. Never before had I so fully appreciated the human will in its greatest power.[137]

Harper's Ferry, W.Va., visited by Lincoln in 1862, occupied and reoccupied by both sides during the Civil War, and preserved today much as it was at that time. (Photo: William A. Bake)

90

When McClellan repeatedly underestimated the size of his army in spite of constant reinforcements, Lincoln exclaimed: "Sending men to his army is like shovelling fleas across a barnyard—not half of them get there."[138]

Lincoln said McClellan reminded him of a rooster that belonged to his old Illinois friend Babb McNabb. Babb had bragged a great deal about the fighting qualities of his bird and it was finally matched with a veteran cock in the New Salem pit. Bets ran high. When the two roosters were thrown into the pit, McNabb's bird took one look at his battle-scarred opponent and fled. At a safe distance he mounted a fence, spread his feathers and crowed lustily. Babb, grimly settling with his creditors, looked over at his bird. "Yes, you little cuss," he said, "You're great on dress parade, but you're not worth a damn in a fight."[139]

Replacing McClellan with "Fighting Joe" Hooker, Lincoln gave him some frontier advice.

In case you find Lee coming to the north of the Rappahannock, I would by no means cross to the south of it. . . . I would not take any risk of being entangled upon the river, like an ox jumped half over a fence and liable to be torn by dogs front and rear without a fair chance to gore one way or kick the other."[140]

On one occasion, when Kentucky was overrun, Ohio, Indiana, and Illinois were alarmed. A self constituted committee of distinguished gentlemen determined to go and advise with the President as to what was best to be done.

The President sat on a revolving chair, looking at every one till they were all done. "Now, gentlemen," he said, "I am going to make you a curious kind of a speech. I announce to you that I am not going to do one single thing that any one of you has asked me to do. But it is due to myself and to you that I should give my reasons." He then from his seat answered each man, taking them in the order in which they spoke, never forgetting a point that any one had made. When he was done, he rose from his chair and said,

"Judge List, this reminds me of an anecdote which I heard a son of yours tell in Burlington in Iowa. He was trying to enforce upon his hearers the truth of the old adage that three moves is worse than a fire. As an illustration he gave an account of a family who started from Western Pennsylvania, pretty well off in this world's goods. But they moved and moved, having less and less every time they moved, till after a while they could carry every thing in one wagon. He said that the chickens of the family got so used to being moved, that whenever they saw the wagon sheets brought out they laid themselves on their backs and crossed their legs, ready to be tied. Now, gentlemen, if I were to listen to every committee that comes in that door, I had just as well cross my hands and let you tie me. Nevertheless, I am glad to see you." He left them in good humor.[141]

It was Lincoln's habit to read the wire messages aloud, and when he came across the name of Jefferson Davis or Robert E. Lee, he would say, "Jeffy D.," or "Bobby" Lee.[142]

A farmer from one of the border counties went to the President on a certain occasion with the complaint that the Union soldiers in passing his farm had helped themselves not only to hay but to his horse; and he hoped the proper officer would be required to consider his claim immediately.

"Why, my good sir," replied Mr. Lincoln, "if I should attempt to consider every such individual case, I should find work enough for twenty Presidents! In my early days, I knew one Jack Chase, who was a lumberman on the Illinois, and, when steady and sober, the best raftsman on the river. It was quite a trick twenty-five years ago to take the logs over the rapids, but he was skillful with a raft, and always kept her straight in the channel. Finally a steamer was put on, and Jack—he's dead now, poor fellow!—was made captain of her. He always used to take the wheel going through the rapids. One day, when the boat was plunging and wallowing along the boiling current, and Jack's utmost vigilance was being exercised to keep her in the narrow channel, a boy pulled his coat-tail and hailed him with:

'Say, Mister Captain! I wish you would just stop your boat a minute—I've lost my apple overboard!' "[143]

When Spain attempted to involve the United States in helping her regain control of rebellious San Domingo, Secretary of State William Seward went to the White House to discuss the situation with Lincoln. The President said it reminded him of the choice a Negro preacher gave a noted sinner in Tennessee. " 'Dar are,' said the preacher, 'two roads befo you, Joe; be careful which ob dem you take. Narrow am de way dat leads straight to destruction. But broad am de way dat leads right to damnation.'

"Joe opened his eyes wide with fright and replied, 'Josh, take which way you please. I'm goin' troo de woods.'

"Let us take to the woods," Lincoln said, "and maintain a strict neutrality with Spain and San Domingo."[144]

When Lincoln fired Simon Cameron, his inept Secretary of War, he asked the Philadelphia patent attorney, George Harding, whom he should appoint to this crucial job. "I had in mind only one man," Harding said, "but you could not and would not appoint him after the outrageous way he behaved toward you in the reaper case."

"Oh," said Lincoln, "you mean Stanton. Now, Mr. Harding, this is not a personal matter. I simply desire what will be the best thing for the country."

Later, when Stanton's ego grew dangerously large as Secretary of War, Lincoln continued to regard him as an individual of real stature. "He's a great man, even if he does know it," he said.[145]

CHAPTER NINE

Lincoln found few things in his presidency as hard to bear as the death of his son Willie in 1862.

In the Spring that year, the President spent several days at Fortress Monroe, awaiting military operations upon the peninsula. As a portion of the Cabinet were with him, that was temporarily the seat of government, and he bore with him constantly the burden of public affairs. His favorite diversion was reading Shakespeare. One day (it happened to be the day before the capture of Norfolk) as he sat reading alone, he called to his aide in the adjoining room—"You have been writing long enough, Colonel; come in here. I want to read you a passage in Hamlet!"

He read the discussion on ambition between Hamlet and his courtiers, and the soliloquy, in which conscience debates a future state. This was followed by passages from Macbeth. Then opening to King John, he read from the third act the passage in which Constance bewails her imprisoned, lost boy.

> "And father cardinal, I have heard
>   you say
> That we shall see and know our friends
>   in heaven;
> If that be true, I shall see my boy
>   again."

Mr. Lincoln said: "Colonel, did you ever dream of a lost friend, and feel that you were holding a sweet communion with that friend, and yet have a sad consciousness that it was not a reality?—just so I dream of my boy Willie." Overcome with emotion, he dropped his head on the table, and sobbed aloud.[146]

Robert M. McBride, a member of the White House guard, recalled another incident that revealed Lincoln's grief.

One night there was an alarm of fire. The White House stables were burning. Those of us who were early on the ground saw a tall and hatless man come running from the direction of the White House. We at once recognized him as Mr. Lincoln. When he reached the boxwood hedge that served as an enclosure to the stables he sprang over it like a deer. As he approached these stables he inquired if the horses had been taken out. On learning that they had not, he asked impatiently why they had not, and with his own hands burst open the stable door. A glance within showed that the whole interior of the stable was in flames and that the rescue of the horses was impossible. Notwithstanding this, he would apparently have

95

tried to enter the burning building had not those standing near caught and restrained him. It suddenly occurred to some one that possibly the stables had been fired for the purpose of bringing him out of the White House to assassinate him. Captain Bennett, of the Union Light Guard, and some others immediately hurried him into the White House, while, by Captain Bennett's orders, with a detail of the men of our Company, I took charge of the entrances, remaining there on duty for several hours.

After posting the sentinels, I went inside. Mr. Lincoln, with others, was standing in the East Room, looking at the still burning stables. He was weeping. Little "Tad," his youngest son, explained his father's emotion. Willie had died a short time before. The stables contained a pony that had belonged to the dead boy. The thought of his dead child had come to Mr. Lincoln's mind as soon as he learned the stables were on fire and he had rushed out to try to save the pony from the flames.[147]

The war rumbled and churned through its second year. Lincoln went on trying to win it and simultaneously to cope with the daily deluge of advice from well-intentioned citizens.

At the White House one day some gentlemen were present from the West, excited and troubled about the commissions or omissions of the Administration. The President heard them patiently, and then replied, "Gentlemen, suppose all the property you were worth was in gold, and you had put it in the hands of Blondin to carry across the Niagara River on a rope. Would you shake the cable, or keep shouting out to him, 'Blondin, stand up a little straighter—Blondin, stoop a little more—go a little faster—lean a little more to the north—lean a little more to the south.' No, you would hold your breath as well as your tongue, and keep your hands off until he was safe over. The Government are carrying an immense weight. Untold treasures are in their hands. They are doing the very best they can. Don't badger them. Keep silence, and we'll get you safe across."[148]

Uncannily Lincoln's sense of himself, his confidence in his ability, grew steadily in spite of the grinding, unrelenting pressure of his war-racked presidency.

Judge Treat mentioned to Mr. Lincoln that he had heard some interesting stories of Washington recently related by Mr. Custis, the General's adopted son, who lived with him at Mount Vernon for eighteen years—among other facts, that Washington was perhaps the strongest man of his day and generation, and that in his youth he was a famous wrestler, never having been thrown. "It is rather a curious thing," Mr. Lincoln said, "but that is exactly my record. I could outlift any man in Southern Illinois when I was young, and I never was thrown. If George was loafing around here now, I should be glad to have a tussle with him, and I rather believe that one of the plain people of Illinois would be able to manage the aristocrat of old Virginia."[149]

Mr. Lincoln's "laugh" stood by itself. The "neigh" of a wild horse on his native prairie is not more undisguised and hearty. A group of gentlemen, among whom was his old Springfield friend and associate, Hon. Isaac N. Arnold, were one day conversing in the passage near his office, while awaiting admission. A congressional delegation had preceded them, and presently an unmistakable voice was heard through the partition, in a burst of mirth. Mr. Arnold remarked, as the sound died away: "That laugh has been the President's life-preserver."[150]

Mr. Lincoln's life was almost devoid of recreation. He sometimes went to the theater, and was particularly fond of a play of Shakespeare well acted. He was so delighted with Hackett in *Falstaff* that he wrote him a letter of warm congratulation which pleased the veteran actor so much that he gave it to the *New York Herald*, which printed it with abusive comments. Hackett was greatly mortified and made suitable apologies; upon which the President wrote to him again in the kindliest manner, saying:

"Give yourself no uneasiness on the subject. I certainly did not expect to see my note in print; yet I have not been shocked by the comments upon it. They are a fair specimen of what has occurred to me through life. I have endured a great deal of ridicule, without much malice, and have received a great deal of kindness, not quite free from ridicule. I am used to it."[151]

Ward Hill Lamon, Lincoln's former law partner, was now the U.S. Marshall for the District of Columbia. He was also one of the men who helped Lincoln escape the gruelling pressure of the presidency.

Lincoln loved simple ballads and ditties, such as the common people sing. No one in the list touched his great heart as did the song, "Twenty Years Ago." Many a time, in the old days of our familiar friendship on the circuit and often at the White House when he and I were alone, have I seen him in tears while I was rendering in my poor way that homely melody. The following verses seemed to affect Mr. Lincoln more deeply than any of the others:

"I've wandered to the village, Tom;
    I've sat beneath the tree
Upon the schoolhouse play-ground,
    that sheltered you and me
But none were left to greet me, Tom,
    and few were left to know
Who played with us upon the green,
    some twenty years ago.

Near by the spring, upon the elm you
    know I cut your name—
Your sweetheart's just beneath it,
    Tom, and you did mine the same
Some heartless wretch has peeled the
    bark—t'was dying, sure but slow
Just as she died whose name you cut,
    some twenty years ago.

My lids have long been dry, Tom, but
    tears came to my eyes;
I thought of her I loved so well, those
    early broken ties;
I visited the old churchyard and took
    some flowers to strew
Upon the graves of those we loved,
    some twenty years ago."[152]

Captain Allen Gentry, who had flat-boated to New Orleans with Lincoln in 1828, and hundreds of others from the area that Lincoln called "the triangular region between the Ohio & Wabash

Lincoln traveled down the Hudson River valley, seen here at dusk, by train on the way to his inauguration. He returned in 1862 to visit West Point for a conference with General Winfield Scott. (Photo: Michael A. Vaccaro/Louis Mercier)

rivers, including my old boyhood home" were on the march. Moving along with those troops was the six by ten foot banner depicting Abe Lincoln the Rail-Splitter. According to James M. Justice, a 16th Battery Indiana Light Artillery private who had been wounded at the second Battle of Bull Run, Southerners hooted every time they saw the banner. Twice Rebels captured it and twice the Hoosiers retook it. An ominous bullet-hole defaced the forehead.[153]

With thumb and forefinger the President grasped the extreme end of the handle of an axe and held it at arm's length—an almost unbelievable feat of strength. "When I was eighteen years of age I could do this," he said. "And I have never seen the day since I could not do it."[154]

CHAPTER TEN

On June 23, 1862, Lincoln, baffled and deeply concerned by the failure of his cautious generals, especially George McClellan, to fight the enemy, traveled to West Point to confer with retired General Winfield Scott, the aged hero of the Mexican War. After a five-hour meeting with Scott on the morning of the twenty-fourth, Lincoln decided to inspect the academy from which so many of his generals had been graduated. The cadet corps were in their summer camp at nearby Fort Clinton. The cadets quickly assembled and passed in review before the President. Then, escorted by the superintendent of the academy, the President and his party "tramped from building to building, from department to stable, from tent to riding school, and from parade ground to barracks." Lincoln asked to meet the ten cadets he had recently named as presidential appointees. He was particularly interested in William H. Upham, who had been left for dead on the battlefield at Bull Run, hospitalized in Richmond, and exchanged for a Confederate prisoner.

A number of radical Republican senators, angry at the defection of West Pointers such as Robert E. Lee and Stonewall Jackson, wanted to close the school. Lincoln's inspection tour was a quiet rebuke to their hysterical extremism.[155]

On October 1, 1862, disturbed by McClellan's failure to pursue Lee's army after the September 16 Union victory at Antietam, Lincoln journeyed from Washington to the headquarters of the Army of the Potomac near the battlefield. In the course of his three-day visit, he reviewed several corps of the huge army. Here is one young recruit's recollection.

Our regiment had marched a long distance in the early morning to reach the reviewing field and then came a long, long wait. I was tired, hungry, and thirsty. But finally there came the sound of bugles and loud cries of "Attention!" from officers. A cloud of dust swept toward us from far down the line, and out of it gradually emerged a great number of field and staff-officers, their horses galloping rapidly. At the head rode Major General George B. McClellan, and at his side a civilian, dressed in black and wearing a high silk hat. The contrast between the latter and those who were attired in all the glittering panoply of war was striking. In the fraction of the moment that my eyes rested on Mr. Lincoln, somehow my heart warmed toward the great man, and I whispered softly to myself: "I'm glad I enlisted."[156]

Lincoln also visited wounded soldiers in nearby churches and public buildings. Several years ago, in an old attendance book of St. Paul's Church in Burkittsville, the Reverend H. Austin Cooper discovered a letter from a Georgia soldier, Benjamin Prather, to his wife. Prather had been wounded and captured during the heavy skirmishes that preceded the Battle of Antietam.

Beloved wife I am not well. On the fourteenth [of September] I got shot in the right knee and hip. Doctor J. Garrott took off my leg above the knee on the eighteenth. My hip smells so bad it is rotten. It thumps and my head and eyes hurt all the time. O beloved Anna Elizabeth I fear I shall never again see you. . . .

Yesterday afternoon there was much commotion here. The Fed General McClellan and Mr. Abraham Lincoln stopped at the German Reform Church and here at St. Paul's. Mr. Lincoln is not a handsome man but he spoke very kindly to us. The [wounded] Feds are in the balcony in both churches and our men are in

Overleaf: *Antietam battlefield.* (*Photo: William A. Bake*)

the pews and on the floor. Mr. Lincoln promised us immediate help. He laid his hand on my shoulder and knelt before the altar and prayed a beautiful short prayer. He seemed to be a right good man.[157]

One of Lincoln's closest friends in Bloomington, Illinois, was William McCullough, who was sheriff and clerk of the McLean County Circuit Court. He was killed leading a night cavalry charge near Coffeeville, Mississippi, on December 5, 1862. Lincoln wrote his daughter a letter which summed up much of his own experience with sorrow.

Executive Mansion,
Washington, December 23, 1862.
Dear Fanny

It is with deep grief that I learn of the death of your kind and brave Father; and, especially, that it is affecting your young heart beyond what is common, in such cases. In this sad world of ours, sorrow comes to all; and, to the young, it comes with bitterest agony, because it takes them unawares. The older have learned to ever expect it. I am anxious to afford some alleviation of your present distress. Perfect relief is not possible, except with time. You can not now realize that you will ever feel better. Is not this so? And yet it is a mistake. You are sure to be happy again. To know this, which is certainly true, will make you some less miserable now. I have had experience enough to know what I say; and you need only to believe it, to feel better at once. The memory of your dear Father, instead of an agony, will yet be a sad sweet feeling in your heart, of a purer and holier sort than you have known before.

Please present my kind regards to your afflicted mother.

Your sincere friend
A. Lincoln[158]

Union soldiers from seventeen states fell at Gettysburg. These states bore the cost of acquiring seventeen acres of the battlefield to be converted into a "National Soldiers' Cemetery." The trustees, composed of one man from each of the states, invited Edward Everett, considered the leading orator of the day, to deliver the memorial address.

When Clark E. Carr, the trustee from Illinois, suggested that the President be requested

The house in Gettysburg
where Lincoln stayed for the
ceremonies dedicating the cemetery.
In this room he revised his
brief but immortal remarks
for the occasion.
(Photo: Fred J. Maroon/Louis Mercier)

Here the crowd stood
to hear Lincoln's Gettysburg Address.
Expecting a longer speech,
the awe-struck people gave no sign
of approval or appreciation
when Lincoln finished.
(Photo: Fred J. Maroon/Louis Mercier)

to speak at the dedicatory ceremonies, other members of the board questioned his ability "to speak upon such a grave and solemn occasion." Not until November 2, more than six weeks after the invitation to Everett, was Lincoln asked to speak at Gettysburg.[159]

During the ride to Gettysburg the President placed every one who approached him at his ease, relating numerous stories, some of them laughable, and others of a character that deeply touched the hearts of his listeners.

I remember well his reply to a gentleman who stated that his "only son fell on 'Little Round Top' and I am going to look at the spot."

President Lincoln replied:

"You have been called upon to make a terrible sacrifice for the Union, and a visit to that spot, I fear, will open your wounds afresh. But oh! my dear sir, if we had reached the end of such sacrifices, and had nothing left for us to do but to place garlands on the graves of those who have already fallen, we could give thanks even amidst our tears; but when I think of the sacrifices of life yet to be offered and the hearts and homes yet to be made desolate before this dreadful war, so wickedly forced upon us, is over, my heart is like lead within me, and I feel at times, like hiding in deep darkness."[160]

At one of the stopping-places of the train, a very beautiful little child, having a bouquet of rose-buds in her hand, was lifted up to an open window of the President's car. With a childish lisp she said: "Flowrth for the President!"

The President stepped to the window, took the rose-buds, bent down and kissed the child, saying:

"'You're a sweet little rose-bud yourself. I hope your life will open into perpetual beauty and goodness."[161]

A day or two before the dedication of the National Cemetery at Gettysburg, Mr. Lincoln told me that he would be expected to make a speech on the occasion; that he was extremely busy and had no time for preparation; that he greatly feared he would not be able to acquit himself with credit, much less to fill the measure of public expectation. From his hat—the usual receptacle for his private notes and memoranda— he drew a sheet of foolscap, one side of which was closely written with what he informed me was a memorandum of his intended address. This he read to me, first remarking that it was not at all satisfactory to him. It proved to be in substance, if not in exact words, what was afterwards printed as his famous Gettysburg speech.

After its delivery on the day of commemoration, he expressed deep regret that he had not prepared it with greater care. He said to me on the stand, immediately after concluding the speech: "Lamon, that speech won't *scour!* It is a flat failure, and the people are disappointed." (The word "scour" he often used in expressing his positive conviction that a thing lacked merit, or would not stand the test of close criticism or the wear of time.)[162]

It seemed that he had but started speaking when, with both arms extended, as if in benediction, he finished and retired without a change in his solemn countenance. No one realized that he had finished, evidently expecting a much longer effort; and the awe-struck people, apparently deeply moved, gave no sign of approval or appreciation.

The profound silence which attended the speech continued; not a sound was heard for a minute or two; then everyone began turning to his neighbors, looking into their faces, and making such comments as, "Did he finish? Was it not a grand speech, but so short!"

Though Everett, Seward and others on the platform shook Mr. Lincoln's hand, he took his seat, evidently sorely disappointed that the people had given no sign of any kind as to the effect of the speech.[163]

It had not occurred to me that he would speak like a Kentuckian, but he did, and his slow, careful enunciation made it the more apparent. I remember especially the long "o" in his preposition "to." He said "dedicated toe the proposition," "we have come toe dedicate a portion of that field."

My next feeling was one of complete surprise at his stopping. It seemed to me and I think to the audience generally that he had just begun. I could hardly believe my eyes when I saw him taking his seat.[164]

Years later, a divinity student who was present at Gettysburg that day explained the crowd's reaction: "The hearts of his hearers were too deeply stirred by feelings that forbade boisterousness. A one armed soldier near me voiced the feelings of the vast audience. With tears streaming down his face, and the handless arm upraised, he exclaimed: "God bless Abe Lincoln.""[165]

CHAPTER ELEVEN

Paul M. Angle somewhere remarks that "Mr. Lincoln was always doing something for somebody." Early in 1864 he remembered a forgotten victim of the struggle against slavery, Calvin Fairbank. A graduate of Oberlin, he began leading slaves to freedom along the underground railroad in the 1840s. He was arrested and sentenced to fifteen years' hard labor in the Kentucky state prison at Frankfort. There, during a twelve-year period, he received on his bared body

more than 35,000 stripes laid on with the strap of half-tanned leather. In 1864, with Union armies in firm control of Kentucky and its loyalty to the Union thus guaranteed, Lincoln sent General Speed S. Fry to the acting governor and told him: "The President thinks it would be well to make this Fairbank's day."[166]

In the White House, the men closest to Lincoln, such as his secretary, John Hay, began to regard him with a kind of awe.

The president is managing this war, the draft, foreign relations, and planning a reconstruction of the Union, all in one. The old man sits here and wields like a backwoods Jupiter the bolts of war and the machinery of the government.[167]

Unlike the old Greek God, this Jupiter had no love for vengeance.

A lawyer from Indiana, Judge McDonald, came to the White House to plead for mercy for some deserters who had been convicted of ambushing a troop of federal cavalry that was pursuing them. Lincoln heard him out, and decided to pardon the men. As McDonald said goodbye, he re-

Detail (enlarged) from the only known photograph of Lincoln at Gettysburg. (Photo: Lloyd Ostendorf)

marked: "Mr. President, you are not the blood-thirsty man you have the reputation for being." The President looked at him a moment or two with his great eyes and then replied: "Judge McDonald, if I were the only butcher in America the people would go a long, long time without meat."[168]

As the war dragged on, newspaper attacks on Lincoln became more and more ferocious. Lincoln said that at times he felt like a traveller on the frontier, who found himself caught on the road in a terrific thunderstorm. He floundered along until his horse at length gave out. The lightning afforded him the only clue to his way, but the peals of thunder were frightful. One bolt, which seemed to crash the earth beneath him, brought him to his knees. By no means a praying man, his petition was short and to the point,—"O Lord, if it is all the same to you, give us a little more light and a little less noise!"[169]

While Lincoln's policies displeased Senators Chandler, Wade, and Sumner, it was Wade who usually was irritated by the President's story-telling. Once Wade came to the White House to urge the President to dismiss General Grant. "Senator," said Lincoln, "that reminds me of a story." Wade interjected: "It is with you, sir, all story, story! You are the father of every military blunder that has been made during the war. You are on your road to hell, sir, with this government. You are not a mile off this minute." Lincoln responded: "Senator, that is just about the distance from here to the Capitol, is it not?"[170]

Attorney-General Bates, who was a Virginian by birth and had many relatives in that State, one day heard that a young Virginian, the son of one of his old friends, had been captured across the Potomac, was a prisoner of war, and was not in good health. Knowing the boy's father to be in his heart a Union man, Mr. Bates conceived the idea of having the son paroled and sent home, of course under promise not to return to the army. He went to see the President and said:

"I have a personal favor to ask. I want you to give me a prisoner."

And he told him of the case. The President said:

"Bates, I have an almost parallel case. The son of an old friend of mine in Illinois ran off and entered the rebel army. The young fool has been captured, is a prisoner of war, and his old broken-hearted father has asked me to send him home, promising of course to keep him there. I have not seen my way clear to do it, but if you and I unite our influence I believe we can manage it together and make two loyal fathers happy."[171]

During the election campaign of 1864, when it looked for a time that Lincoln would be defeated, he sent a message to an old friend in Petersburg, the town that had absorbed New Salem, reminding him that he had once rescued him in a fight with a bully. "Tell Clark I stood by him in a fight he once had in New Salem and I am in a big fight now and I want him to stand by me."[172]

Toward the end of the war Senator John A. S. Creswell of Maryland came to Lincoln to request the release of an old friend who had been captured and imprisoned. "I know the man has acted like a fool," admitted Creswell, "but he is my friend, and a good fellow; let him out; give him to me, and I will be responsible that he will have nothing further to do with the rebels." Lincoln pondered the matter. The request brought to his mind a group of young people who went "Maying." In the course of their rambles they crossed a shallow stream in a flatboat, but on their return they discovered that the boat was gone. So each boy picked up a girl and carried her across, until the only ones remaining were a little short chap and a great "Gothic-built" old maid. "Now, Creswell," complained Lincoln, "you are trying to leave me in the same predicament. You fellows are all getting your friends out of this scrape; and you will succeed in carrying off one after another, until nobody but Jeff Davis and myself will be left, and then I won't know what to do. How should I feel? How should I look, lugging him over?"[173]

Only to his closest friends such as Joshua Speed did Lincoln reveal his growing exhaustion. Yet he somehow managed to control his weariness, to remain in touch with his better nature.

He sent me word by my brother James, then in his Cabinet, that he desired to see me before I went home. I went into his office about eleven o'clock. Across the fire-place from him, sat two humble-looking women. Seeing them there seemed to provoke him, and he said, "Well, ladies, what can I do for you?" One was an old woman, the other young. They both commenced talking at once. The President soon comprehended them. "I suppose," said he, "that your son and your husband are in prison for resisting the draft in Western Pennsylvania. Where is your petition?" The old lady replied, "Mr. Lincoln, I've got no petition. I went to a lawyer to get one drawn, and I had not the money to pay him and come here too; so, I thought I would just come and ask you to let me have my boy." "And it's your husband you want?" said he, turning to the young woman. "Yes," said she.

He rung his bell and called his servant, and bade him to go and tell Gen. Dana to bring him the list of prisoners for resisting the draft in Western Pennsylvania.

The General soon came, bringing a package of papers. The President opened it, and, counting the names, said, "General, there are twenty-seven of these men. Is there any difference in degree of their guilt?" "No," said the General.

"Well, said the President, looking out of the window and seemingly talking to himself, "these poor fellows have, I think, suffered enough; they have been in prison fifteen months. I have been thinking so for some time, and have so said to Stanton, and he always threatened to resign if they are released. But he has said so about other matters, and never did. So now, while I have the paper in my hand, I will turn out the flock." So he wrote, "Let the prisoners named in the within paper be discharged," and signed it. The General made his bow and left. Then, turning to the ladies, he said, "Now ladies, you can go. Your son, madam, and your husband, madam, is free."

The young woman ran across to him and began to kneel. He took her by the elbow and said, impatiently, "Get up, get up; none of this." But the old woman walked to him, wiping with her apron the tears that were coursing down her cheeks. She gave him her hand, and looking into his face said, "Good-bye, Mr. Lincoln, we will never meet again till we meet in Heaven." A change came over his sad and weary face. He clasped her hand in both of his, and followed her to the door, saying as he went, "With all that I have to cross me here, I am afraid that I will never get there; but your wish that you will meet me there has fully paid for all I have done for you."

We were then alone. He drew his chair to the fire and said, "Speed, I am a little alarmed about myself; just feel my hand." It was cold and clammy.

He pulled off his boots, and, putting his feet to the fire, the heat made them steam. I said overwork was producing nervousness. "No," said he, "I am not tired." "Such a scene as I have just witnessed is enough to make you nervous," I said. "How much you are mistaken," said he; "I have made two people happy to-day; I have given a mother her son, and a wife her husband. That young woman is a counterfeit, but the old woman is a true mother."[174]

Despite those acts of mercy, however, and despite his public acknowledgment that he considered himself an instrument of Providence and relied for guidance upon a Higher Power, Lincoln's enemies raised the cry that he had no religion. Without rancor he answered them: "My religion is like that of an old man named Glenn, in Indiana, whom I heard speak at a church meeting. 'When I do good, I feel good; when I do bad I feel bad. And that's my religion.' "[175]

As the Confederacy neared collapse, Lincoln called a cabinet meeting and asked each member his opinion of what should be done with captured rebel leaders. Most of them were for hanging the traitors, or for some severe punishment. Lincoln said nothing. Finally Joshua F. Speed, his old and confidential friend, said: "I have heard the opinions of your ministers, and would like to hear yours."

"Well, Josh," replied Lincoln, "when I was a boy in Indiana, I went to a neighbor's house one morning and found a boy of my own size holding a coon by a string. I asked him what he was doing. He said: 'Dad cotched six last night and killed all but this poor little cuss. Dad told me to hold him until he came back, and I'm afraid he's going to kill this one too. Oh, Abe, I do wish he would get away.' 'Well, why don't you let him loose?' I said. 'If I let him go, Dad would give me hell. But if he would get away himself, it would be all right.'

"Now," said Lincoln, "if Jeff Davis and those other fellows will only get away, it will be all right. But if we should catch them and I should let them go, 'Dad would give me hell.' "[176]

"Fellow citizens, we cannot escape history," Lincoln had told Americans, north and south. In his quiet, calm way Lincoln demonstrated one of the central meanings of that profound truth when he invited ex-slave Frederick Douglass to the White House.

For the first time in my life, and I suppose the first time in any colored man's life, I attended the reception of a president on the evening of the inauguration. As I approached the door I was seized by two policemen and forbidden to enter. I said to them that they were mistaken entirely in what they were doing, that if Mr. Lincoln knew that I was at the door he would order my admission, and I bolted in by them. On the inside I was taken charge of by two other policemen to be conducted as I supposed to the President, but instead they were conducting me out the window on a plank.

"Oh," said I, "this will not do," and to a gentleman passing in I said, "Just say to Mr. Lincoln that Fred Douglass is at the door."

He rushed in to President Lincoln, and in less than half a minute I was invited into the East Room of the White House. A perfect sea of beauty and elegance it was. The ladies were in very fine attire, and Mrs. Lincoln was standing there. I could not have been more than ten feet from him when Mr. Lincoln saw me; his countenance lighted up, and he said in a voice which was heard all around: "Here comes my friend Douglass." As I approached him he reached out his hand, gave me a cordial shake, and said: "Douglass, I saw you in the crowd today listening to my inaugural address. There is no man's opinion that I value more than yours; what do you think of it?" I said, "Mr. Lincoln, I cannot stop here to talk with you, as there are thousands waiting to shake you by the hand." But he said again: "What did you think of it?" I said: "Mr. Lincoln, it was a sacred effort." "I am glad you liked it," he said. That was the last time I saw him.[177]

On March 23, 1865, Lincoln, his wife, and their son Tad took a steamboat down to City Point (now Hopewell) Virginia, where the Union Army had established a huge supply base. General Ulysses S. Grant had his temporary field headquarters on a nearby bluff. The southern armies were nearing collapse, and Lincoln wanted to press Grant and his other generals onward to victory. The President stayed at City Point until April 3, conferring with Grant, Sherman, and Sheridan on plans for the last campaign, listening to the thunder of Grant's guns as he launched the final assault on the defenses of Richmond. On April 13 Grant telegraphed that Richmond had fallen. Lincoln decided to visit the Confederate capital and sailed up the James River on a U.S. Navy gunboat. A Boston reporter described his arrival.

Such a hurly-burly—such wild, indescribable ecstatic joy I never witnessed. Six sailors, wearing their round blue caps and short jackets and bagging pants, with navy carbines, was the advance guard. Then came the President and Admiral Porter, flanked by the officers accompanying him, and the correspondent of *The Journal,* then six more sailors with carbines—twenty of us all told—amid a surging mass of men, women and children, black, white, and yellow, running, shouting, dancing, swinging their caps, bonnets and handkerchiefs. The soldiers saw him and swelled the crowd, cheering in wild enthusiasm. All could see him, he was so tall, so conspicuous.

One coloured woman, standing in a doorway, as the President passed along the sidewalk, shouted, "Thank you, dear Jesus, for this! thank you, Jesus!" Another standing by her side was clapping her hands and shouting, "Bless de Lord!"

A coloured woman snatched her bonnet from her head whirled it in the air, screaming with all her might. "God bless you, Massa Linkum!"

A few white women looking out from the houses waved their handkerchiefs. One lady in a large and elegant building looked awhile, and then turned away her head as if it was a disgusting sight.

President Lincoln walked in silence, acknowledging the salutes of officers and soldiers and of the citizens, black and white. It was the man of the people among the people. It was the great deliverer, meeting the delivered. Yesterday morning the majority of the thousands who crowded the streets and hindered our advance were slaves. Now they were free, and beheld him who had given their liberty.[178]

George Pickett, who led the famous southern charge at Gettysburg, had been appointed to West Point by Congressman Lincoln. Pickett had been living in Illinois at the time. Now, as Lincoln toured Richmond, someone pointed out Pickett's house. He got out of the carriage and knocked on the door. Mrs. Pickett tells the rest of the story.

Hearing a knock I opened the door with my baby in my arms and saw a tall, gaunt, and sad-faced man who asked:

"Is this George Pickett's place?"

"Yes, sir, but he is not here."

"I know that, ma'am, but I just wanted to see the place. Down in old Quincy, Ill. I have heard the lad describe the home. I am Abraham Lincoln."

"The President," I gasped.

The stranger shook his head.

"No, ma'am; just Abraham Lincoln. George Pickett's old boyhood friend."

"I am George Pickett's wife and this is his boy."

I had never seen Mr. Lincoln but remembered the intense love and reverence with which my soldier always spoke of him.

It had been long since my baby had seen a man and being reminded of his own father, reached out his hands to Mr. Lincoln, who took him in his arms. My baby gave his father's friend a dewy kiss. Putting the little one back in my arms, Mr. Lincoln said:

"Tell your father, the rascal, that I forgive him for the sake of that kiss and those bright eyes."[179]

*On Good Friday, April 14, 1865,
while attending Ford's Theatre,
Lincoln was assassinated.
The theatre has been restored,
outside and in, to look
as it did on that fatal night.
(Photo: Fred J. Maroon/Louis Mercier)*

*The Presidential Box.
(Photo: Fred J. Maroon/Louis Mercier)*

Returning from Richmond, he stopped at City Point (outside Washington) and said he wished to shake hands with every soldier in the hospitals there. As the tall figure appeared, he was recognized by a wounded Rebel who extended his hand and exclaimed, while tears ran down his cheeks: "Mr. Lincoln, I have long wanted to see you to ask your forgiveness for ever raising my hand against the Old Flag." Mr. Lincoln was also moved to tears as he heartily shook the hand.[180]

CHAPTER TWELVE

On Palm Sunday, April 9, 1865, Robert E. Lee surrendered his Army of Northern Virginia to Ulysses S. Grant. After so many years of grief and frustration and defeat, Lincoln's hopes—and the nation's—soared as Union armies closed in on the remaining Confederate forces. On Good Friday morning, April 14, 1865, he wrote a letter to a man who had sent him advice on the coming problems of reconstruction.

Washington, April 14th, 1865.
. . . I thank you for the assurance you give me that I shall be supported by conservative men like yourself, in the efforts I may make to restore the Union, so as to make it, to use your language, a Union of hearts and hands as well as of states. Yours truly,

A. Lincoln[181]

That night, while attending Ford's Theater, Lincoln was assassinated by the actor John Wilkes Booth. Recently the Massachusetts Historical Society acquired a hitherto-unknown letter by an eyewitness of the crime.

Ordnance Office,
War Department
Washington
April 16, 1865

Dear Uncle
You have of course heard all the particulars of the dreadful death of the President of the 14th inst. But as I was an eye Witness of the latter part I will endeavor to explain matters. At 10¼ Oclock I was looking out of a window of a house opposite the Theatre and seeing a large excited

Funeral Train, bearing the body of Prest Lincoln

Taken at Harrisburgh Penn.

from Washington City to Springfield, Ill.

The funeral train at Harrisburg, Pennsylvania (April 21–22, 1865)
on its way from Washington to Springfield. (Photo: Lloyd Ostendorf)

crowd rush from it I thinking some one might have been robbed ran down stairs and across the street into the theatre and then heard the awful words, "Lincoln is shot"—I sprang off towards the stage over the seats every one being in the wildest commotion and on reaching it saw a lady reaching over the right hand box second tier it was the daughter of Senator Harris of N.Y. I clambered up seized her hand and drew myself into the box and there on the floor lay Abraham Lincoln dying:—his wife near him shrieking and moaning. Major Rathburn and a few others near bye. Several of us lifted him and carried him out in the street and finding his carriage gone I said "take him across the street" he was carried into the house I had just left, and deposited on a bed, his clothes stripped off:—he was shot in the head on a line with the left ear about 2 inches towards the back of the head, the Ball was round and entered about three inches in a line towards the right eye—he was breathing very heavily and his pulse fluctuated from 105 to 42 in about three hours. The blood soon began to settle under his left eye and blackened the whole side of his face. Mrs. Lincoln soon came over and was hardly sane all night and is now quite low. Laura Keene [the actress] came over with her but did not stop—his [son Robert] came in about Eleven and was much agitated. Soon all the members of the Cabinet rushed in with grief and terror depicted on their faces; many Senators and members [of Congress] arrived during the night—the street was cleared of all strangers and a great military force stationed around the square. Stanton was there issuing orders to all parts of the union. . . . Mrs. Lincon came into the room seven times during the night and felt dreadfully she fainted twice and fell over onto the floor. I remained in the room all night long and did all I could to help the best surgeons were there but no attempt was made to extricate the Ball as he was pronounced fatally wounded at first examination he lingered on 'till seven twenty "ano" [sic] when he breathed his last in presence of the members of the Cabinet several senators and others Mrs. Lincoln was not in the room at the time of his death. The body at nine oclock was taken to the White House and has been im-

Along the route of the funeral train, an Illinois landscape. Lincoln still lives in the land he loved. The land still lives in the story of Lincoln's life. (Photo: Arthur Shay)

balmed I got a lock of his hair and a towel saturated with the blood of the best man that ever was President and a friend of the South. . . .

[Augustus Clark][182]

"Tad" was frantic with grief upon being told that his father had been shot. For twenty-four hours the little fellow was perfectly inconsolable. Sunday morning, however, the sun rose in unclouded splendor, and in his simplicity he looked upon this as a token his father was happy. "Do you think my father has gone to heaven?" he asked a gentleman who had called upon Mrs. Lincoln. "I have no doubt of it," was the reply. "Then," he exclaimed in his broken way, "I am glad he has gone there, for he never was happy after he came here. This was not a good place for him!"[183]

On Goosenest Prairie, Lincoln's cousin and boyhood playmate Dennis Hanks told Sarah Bush Lincoln the news.

I had to go out to the farm to tell Aunt Sairy. Tom'd been dead a good while, an' she was livin' on thar, alone.

"Aunt Sairy," sez I, "Abe's dead."

"Yes, I know, Denny. I knowed they'd kill him. I ben awaitin' fur it," an' she never asked no questions. She was gettin' purty old, an' I reckon she thought she'd jine him. She never counted on seein' him agin after he went down to Washington, no how."[184]

After being mourned in Washington, Lincoln's body was placed aboard a train that slowly made its way west to Springfield. Among the many ceremonies along the route, one of the most moving took place in the town of Lincoln, Illinois.

Minute guns, fife and muffled drum, greeted the train, just as the sun arose in splendor over the prairie. A large number of people had assembled and portraits of Lincoln with emblems of mourning were everywhere visible. Among the mottoes displayed were: "Mournfully, tenderly, bear him to his grave," and "He saved our country and freed a race." The depot was draped in mourning, and ladies dressed in white, trimmed with black, sang a requiem, as the train passed under a handsomely constructed arch, on each column of which was a portrait of the deceased President. The arch bore the motto: "With malice to none, with charity for all."[185]

On the right-of-way of the New York Central Railroad, track-walkers, sand-house men, "shacks" and section-hands used to tell this story:

"Regularly in the month of April, about midnight the air on the tracks becomes very keen and cutting. On either side of the tracks it is warm and still. Every watchman, when he feels the air, slips off the track and sits down to watch. Soon the pilot engine of Lincoln's funeral train passes with long, black streamers and with a band of black instruments playing dirges, grinning skeletons sitting all about.

"It passes noiselessly. If it is moonlight, clouds come over the moon as the phantom train goes by. After the pilot engine passes, the funeral train itself with flags and streamers rushes past. The track seems covered with black carpet, and the coffin is seen in the center of the car, while all about it in the air and on the train behind are vast numbers of blue-coated men, some with coffins on their backs, others leaning upon them.

"If a real train were passing its noise would be hushed as if the phantom train rode over it. Clocks and watches always stop as the phantom train goes by and when looked at are five to eight minutes behind."[186]

Newspaperman Donn Piatt, who knew Lincoln, believed he had played a unique role in America's history.

"Washington taught the world to know us, Lincoln taught us to know ourselves."[187]

A young New Hampshire woman, Edna Dean Proctor, voiced the devotion of those of her state where Lincoln had won such admiration in his 1860 visit.

Not for thy sheaves nor savannas
Crown we thee, proud Illinois!
Here in his grave is thy grandeur,
Born of his sorrow thy joy.
Only the tomb by Mount Zion

Hewn for the Lord do we hold
Dearer than his in thy prairies,
Girdled with harvests of gold.[188]

Noblest and truest of all the poetic tributes was the close of James Russell Lowell's ode.

Great captains, with their guns and
drums,
Disturb our judgment for the hour.
But at last silence comes;
These all are gone, and, standing like a
tower,
Our children shall behold his fame.
The kindly-earnest, brave, foreseeing
man,
Sagacious, patient, dreading praise, not
blame,
New birth of our new soil, the first
American.[189]

While traveling in the Caucasus Tolstoi was the guest of a Circassian chief who lived in a remote mountain region. After they had talked awhile the devout Mussulman wanted to hear about the "outside world." But it was not until Tolstoi started to talk about great leaders that the chief showed an interest. At that point he interrupted to call in others to listen. When Tolstoi had finished, the tall, gray-bearded chief said:

"But you have not told us about the greatest ruler of the world. We want to know something about him. He was a hero. He spoke with a voice of thunder, he laughed like the sunrise and his deeds were strong as the rock and as sweet as the fragrance of roses. . . . He was so great that he even forgave the crimes of his greatest enemies and shook brotherly hands with those who had plotted against his life. His name was Lincoln and the country in which he lived is called America. . . . Tell us of that man."

Tolstoi told them all he knew of Lincoln.[190]

At Elmhurst, Illinois, Carl Sandburg once asked the ancient Irish flagman of the Chicago, Aurora & Elgin Railroad, how he would explain, in a few words, why Lincoln was loved by so many people.

"He was humanity," said the flagman.[191]

"Now he belongs to the ages."
(*Photo: Fred J. Maroon/Louis Mercier*)

NOTES

1. Ida Tarbell, *In The Footsteps of the Lincolns* (New York: Harper & Brothers, 1924), p. 95.
2. Louis A. Warren, "Environs of Lincoln's Youth," Abraham Lincoln Association Papers (1933), p. 119.
3. Edwin Markham, "Lincoln, Man of the People," in *Lincoln and the Poets,* William W. Betts, Jr., ed. (University of Pittsburgh: Pittsburgh Press, 1965). Permission of Virgil Markham.
4. Eleanor Atkinson, *The Boyhood of Lincoln* (New York: The McClure Co., 1907), p. 11.
5. Henry B. Kranz, ed., *Abraham Lincoln, A New Portrait* (New York: Putnam's, 1959), p. 159.
6. Tarbell, *op. cit.,* p. 102.
7. Atkinson, *op. cit.,* p. 13.
8. Robert W. McBride, *Personal Recollections of Abraham Lincoln* (Indianapolis: Bobbs-Merrill, 1926), pp. 18–24.
9. Tarbell, *op. cit.,* p. 105.
10. *Ibid.,* p. 119.
11. Roy P. Basler, ed., *Collected Works of Abraham Lincoln* (New Brunswick, N.J.: Rutgers University Press, 1953–55), Vol. I, p. 386.
12. E. S. Miers, ed., Lincoln Day by Day (Washington, D.C.: Lincoln Sesquicentennial Commission, 1960), Vol. I, p. 71.
13. Atkinson, *op. cit.,* p. 18.
14. Louis A. Warren, *Lincoln's Youth* (New York: Appleton–Century–Crofts, 1959), p. 83.
15. Tarbell, *op. cit.,* p. 125.
16. Manuscript, Library of Congress. Cited in Edward J. Kempf, *Abraham Lincoln's Philosophy of Common Sense* (New York: Academy of Medicine, 1965), Vol. I, p. 80.
17. Atkinson, *op. cit.,* pp. 26–27.
18. Francis M. Van Natter, *Lincoln's Boyhood* (Washington, D.C.: Public Affairs Press, 1963), p. 41.
19. Thomas D. Jones, *Memories of Lincoln* (New York: The Press of the Pioneers, Inc., 1934), p. 15.
20. Van Natter, *op. cit.,* pp. 41–42.
21. Stephen B. Oates, *With Malice Towards None* (New York: Harper & Row, 1977), p. 12.
22. Kempf, *op. cit.,* p. 88.
23. Van Natter, *op. cit.,* p. 31.
24. Warren, *op. cit.,* pp. 179–80.
25. *Ibid.,* p. 182.
26. William Herndon and Jesse W. Weik, *Abraham Lincoln* (New York: Appleton, 1888), Vol. I, p. 67.
27. Atkinson, *op. cit.,* p. 41.
28. Tarbell, *op. cit.,* p. 158.
29. Ward H. Lamon, *The Life of Abraham Lincoln* (Boston: J. B. Osgood, 1872), pp. 83–84.
30. Henry B. Rankin, *Intimate Character Sketches of Abraham Lincoln* (Philadelphia: Lippincott, 1924), p. 32.
31. Lamon, *op. cit.,* pp. 91–92.
32. *Ibid.,* p. 94.
33. Benjamin P. Thomas, *Lincoln's New Salem* (Springfield, Ill: The Abraham Lincoln Association, 1934), pp. 45–46.
34. Paul Angle and Earl S. Miers, eds., *The Living Lincoln* (New Brunswick, N.J.: Rutgers University Press, 1955), p. 9.
35. Rexford Newcomb, *In The Lincoln Country* (Philadelphia: Lippincott, 1928), p. 105.
36. Thomas, *op. cit.,* p. 33.
37. Tarbell, *op. cit.,* p. 199.
38. Thomas, *op. cit.,* p. 81 ff.
39. D. B. Carpenter, *Six Months at the White House with Lincoln* (Watkins Glen, N.Y.: Century House, 1961—orig, pub. 1866), pp. 25–26. Also Kempf, *op. cit.,* pp. 135–36.
40. Rankin, *op. cit.,* p. 250.
41. Tarbell, *op. cit.,* p. 223.
42. John J. Duff, *A. Lincoln, Prairie Lawyer* (New York: Rinehart & Co., 1960), p. 198.
43. Rufus Rockwell Wilson, ed., *Intimate Memories of Lincoln* (Elmira, N.Y.: The Primavera Press, Inc., 1945), pp. 92–93.
44. Emmanuel Hertz, *Lincoln Talks* (New York: Viking Press, 1939), p. 80.
45. *Ibid.,* p. 84.
46. Duff, *op. cit.,* p. 252.
47. Henry C. Whitney, *Life on the Circuit with Lincoln* (Boston: Estes & Lauriat, 1892), p. 132.
48. *Ibid.,* p. 9.
49. Ward Hill Lamon, *Recollections of Lincoln* (Chicago: A. C. McClurg, 1895), p. 19.
50. Wilson, *op. cit.,* p. 106.

51. Duff, *op. cit.,* p. 349.
52. Charles H. Coleman, *Abraham Lincoln and Coles County, Illinois* (New Brunswick, N.J.: Scarecrow Press, 1955), p. 67.
53. Duff, *op. cit.,* pp. 192–93.
54. James Russell Lowell, "Ode Recited at the Harvard Commemoration," in Betts, *op. cit.*
55. J. F. Speed, *Reminiscences of Abraham Lincoln* (Louisville, Ky.: J. P. Morton & Co., 1884), p. 25.
56. Duff, *op. cit.,* p. 355.
57. *Ibid.,* pp. 323–24.
58. *Ibid.,* pp. 332–44.
59. Richard F. Lufkin, "Mr. Lincoln's Light from Under a Bushel," *Lincoln Herald* (Harrogate, Tenn., Winter 1953), p. 11.
60. Paul M. Angle, "Lincoln: Self Biographer," *Abraham Lincoln Quarterly,* No. 3 (September 1960), p. 155.
61. A. L. Bowen, "A. Lincoln: His House," Abraham Lincoln Association Papers (1925), p. 43.
62. *Ibid.,* p. 63.
63. Albert J. Beveridge, *Abraham Lincoln* (Boston: Houghton Mifflin, 1928), Vol. II, p. 69.
64. Katherine Helm, *Mary, Wife of Lincoln* (New York: Harper & Bros., 1928), p. 112.
65. Rankin, *op. cit.,* p. 100.
66. Benjamin P. Thomas, "Lincoln's Humor," Abraham Lincoln Association Papers (1936), p. 75.
67. Coleman, *op. cit.,* p. 115.
68. Herndon and Weik, *op. cit.,* p. 88.
69. Rankin, *op. cit.,* pp. 46–48.
70. *Collected Works,* Vol. I, p. 430.
71. *Ibid.,* p. 473.
72. *Ibid.,* p. 484.
73. Allen T. Rice, ed., *Reminiscences of Lincoln* (New York: Harper & Bros., 1909), p. 96.
74. Angle and Miers, *op. cit.,* p. 116.
75. *Ibid.,* p. 210.
76. Harry E. Pratt, ed., *Illinois as Lincoln Knew It* (Springfield, Ill: Illinois State Historical Society, 1937), pp. 33–34.
77. Helm, *op. cit.,* p. 100.
78. "This Side of the Mountains, Abraham Lincoln's 1848 Visit to Massachusetts," *Lincoln Herald* (Harrogate, Tenn., Summer 1978), p. 56.
79. *Ibid.,* p. 58.
80. *Ibid.*
81. Tarbell, *op. cit.,* p. 287.
82. "This Side of the Mountains," *op. cit.,* p. 69.
83. *Collected Works,* Vol. II, pp. 10–11.
84. John W. Starr, *Lincoln and the Railroads* (New York: Dodd, Mead, 1927), pp. 100–01.
85. *Collected Works,* Vol. II, p. 97.
86. Joseph J. Lewis, *Lincoln's Kalamazoo Address* (Detroit: Detroit Fine Books Circle, 1941), pp. 31, 45. (Reprinted from Bulletin No. 34, William L. Clement Library, University of Michigan.)
87. *Collected Works,* Vol. II, p. 320.
88. Rankin, *op. cit.,* pp. 123–24.
89. Paul Sigelschiffer, *The American Conscience* (New York: Horizon Press, 1973), pp. 173–74.
90. *Collected Works,* Vol. II, p. 452; Herndon and Weik, *op. cit.,* p. 69 for President quote.
91. Tarbell, *op. cit.,* p. 356.
92. Angle and Miers, *op. cit.,* p. 273.
93. Lamon, *op. cit.,* p. 24.
94. Wilson, *op. cit.,* p. 148.
95. Ruth P. Randall, *Mary Lincoln* (Boston: Little Brown, 1953), pp. 171–72.
96. Herndon and Weik, *op. cit.,* Vol. II, pp. 7–8.
97. John H. Morgan, *Lincoln's Last Speech in Springfield* (Chicago: University of Chicago Press, 1925), p. 22.
98. *Collected Works,* Vol. III, p. 203.
99. William Richardson, *The Makings of the Lincoln Association of Jersey City* (Jersey City, N.J.: Jersey City Printing Co., 1919), p. 6.
100. Hertz, *op. cit.,* p. 165.
101. Starr, *op. cit.,* p. 196.
102. Wilson, *op. cit.,* pp. 212–13.
103. *Collected Works,* Vol. III, p. 504.
104. Anna Lux, Staff Memorandum, Rock County Wisconsin Historical Society, p. 3.
105. *Collected Works,* Vol. III, p. 482.
106. Wilson, *op. cit.,* p. 209.
107. Andrew A. Freeman, *Abraham Lincoln Goes to New York* (New York: Coward–McCann, 1960), p. 82.
108. *Ibid.,* p. 75.
109. Rankin, *op. cit.,* p. 186.
110. Freeman, *op. cit.,* pp. 87–88.
111. *Ibid.,* pp. 65–66.
112. Starr, *op. cit.,* pp. 127–28.
113. Percy C. Eggleston, *Lincoln in New England* (New York: Stewart Warren & Co., 1922), pp. 7–8.
114. Edwin L. Page, *Abraham Lincoln in New Hampshire* (Boston: Houghton Mifflin, 1929), pp. 120–24.

115. *Ibid.*, p. 126. Statement by Marshall Snow.
116. *Ibid.*, p. 127. Statement by Albert Blair.
117. George W. Browne, *The Amoskeag Manufacturing Co., A History* (Published by AMC, 1915), pp. 156–57.
118. Eggleston, *op. cit.*, p. 12.
119. *Collected Works*, Vol. IV, p. 24.
120. Paul M. Angle, ed., *Abraham Lincoln by Some Men Who Knew Him* (Freeport, N.Y.: Books for Libraries Press, 1969), pp. 66–67.
121. Henry B. Rankin, *Personal Recollections of Abraham Lincoln* (New York: Putnam's, 1915), pp. 189–90.
122. Coleman, *op. cit.*, pp. 198–99.
123. *Ibid.*, p. 207.
124. Herndon and Weik, *op. cit.*, p. 190.
125. Coleman, *op. cit.*, p. 207.
126. Starr, *op. cit.*, p. 174.
127. Rankin, *Intimate Sketches*, pp. 275–77.
128. *Collected Works*, Vol. IV, p. 219.
129. *Lincoln Herald* (Winter 1958), p. 129.
130. *Collected Works*, Vol. IV, p. 240.
131. Herndon and Weik, *op. cit.*, Vol. II, pp. 208–10.
132. Thomas, *Lincoln's Humor*, p. 69.
133. "Lincoln's Genius of Places," Abraham Lincoln Association Papers (1933), p. 21.
134. Rexford Newcomb, *In the Lincoln Country* (Philadelphia: Lippincott, 1928), p. 110.
135. Thomas, *Lincoln's Humor*, p. 68.
136. Lamon, *Recollections*, pp. 97–98.
137. Wilson, *op. cit.*, pp. 233–34.
138. Whitney, *op. cit.*, p. 183.
139. Thomas, *Lincoln's New Salem*, p. 47.
140. *Collected Works*, Vol. VI, p. 249.
141. Speed, *op. cit.*, pp. 29–30.
142. David H. Bates, *Lincoln's Stories* (New York: William E. Rudge, Inc., 1926), p. 14.
143. Carpenter, *op. cit.*, p. 41.
144. Lamon, *Recollections*, p. 135.
145. Duff, *op. cit.*, p. 324.
146. Carpenter, *op. cit.*, p. 46.
147. McBride, *op. cit.*, pp. 44–46.
148. Carpenter, *op. cit.*, pp. 53–54.
149. Wilson, *op. cit.*, p. 419.
150. Carpenter, *op. cit.*, p. 49.
151. Wilson, *op. cit.*, pp. 400–01.
152. Lamon, *Recollections*, pp. 147–48.
153. Van Natter, *op. cit.*, p. 189.
154. *Ibid.*, p. 170.
155. Thomas Fleming, *West Point* (New York: Morrow, 1969), p. 167; also memorandum from USMA assistant archivist Kenneth W. Rapp in author's file.
156. Wilson, *op. cit.*, p. 485.
157. Memorandum from J. W. Schildt, Chewsville, Md., in author's file.
158. *Collected Works*, Vol. VI, p. 16.
159. Abraham Lincoln, 1809–1959; exhibition at Library of Congress; published by L of C (1959), p. 64.
160. Rice, *op. cit.*, pp. 296–97.
161. *Ibid.*, p. 297.
162. Lamon, *Recollections*, p. 171.
163. William E. Barton, *Lincoln at Gettysburg* (Indianapolis: Bobbs–Merrill, 1930), pp. 188–89.
164. *Ibid.*, pp. 192–93.
165. Junius B. Remensnyder, "With Lincoln at Gettysburg," *Magazine of History* (Vol. 32, no. 125–6, 1926), p. 11.
166. Wilson, *op. cit.*, pp. 6–7.
167. Van Natter, *op. cit.*, p. 173.
168. Wilson, *op. cit.*, p. 274.
169. Carpenter, *op. cit.*, p. 60.
170. Van Natter, *op. cit.*, p. 185.
171. Rice, *op. cit.*, pp. 200–01.
172. Rankin, *Intimate Sketches*, p. 33.
173. Thomas, *Lincoln's Humor*, p. 87.
174. Speed, *op. cit.*, pp. 27–28.
175. Van Natter, *op. cit.*, p. 167.
176. Lamon, *Recollections*, pp. 243–44.
177. Rice, *op. cit.*, p. 322.
178. Herbert R. Mitgang, ed., *A. Lincoln, A Press Portrait* (New York: Quadrangle Books, 1971), pp. 452–53.
179. Fleming, *op. cit.*, pp. 109–10, 205–06.
180. Carpenter, *op. cit.*, p. 188.
181. *Collected Works*, Vol. VIII, p. 413.
182. Massachusetts Historical Society, reprinted with permission.
183. Carpenter, *op. cit.*, p. 78.
184. Coleman, *op. cit.*, p. 154.
185. Lawrence B. Stringer, *History of Logan County, Illinois* (Chicago, 1911), p. 230.
186. Lloyd Lewis, *Myths After Lincoln* (New York: Press of the Reader's Club, 1929), pp. 344–45.
187. Rice, *op. cit.*, p. 366. Statement by Donn Piatt.
188. Page, *op. cit.*, p. 141.
189. Betts, *op. cit.*, p. 33.
190. Kranz, *op. cit.*, p. 171. Statement by Arnold Gates.
191. Lewis, *op. cit.*, p. 344.